Personal Finance

PERSONAL FINANCE

A Practical Guide to Obtain Your Financial Independence and Retire Well

JOSÉ ANTONIO GARNHAM

PERSONAL FINANCE
A Practical Guide to Obtain Your Financial Independence and Retire Well
José Antonio Garnham

Personal Finance is available at special quantity discounts for bulk purchases for sales promotions, fund-raising, educational or institutional use. Special book excerpts or customized printings can also be created to fit specific needs. For details, write or phone the office of Garnham Books.

GARNHAM BOOKS
Email: jagarnham@comcast.net
Website: www.finanzasfamiliares1.com

Books are printed and distributed by Amazon.com

ISBN: 978-0-578-55000-8

TABLE OF CONTENT

FOREWORD

The need for financial education in the 21st century. All human activities have a financial impact. Achieve your independence and financial security for yourself and your family. xv

INTRODUCTION

The importance of family income: two incomes. The goal is to obtain independence and economic security at retirement age or sooner if possible. How much is the minimum I need to retire in dignity? Social Security and Medicare. Retirement fund. Emergency fund. Do not have debts. Have the house paid and free of obligations. Have good health. Income strategy. Expense strategy. Savings strategy. Investment strategy.. . . . xvii

GOAL 1: SOCIAL SECURITY AND MEDICARE

A supplementary income to your pension fund. Requirements to earn Social Security income. Contributions. Benefits. Retirement pension. Disability pension. Widow/widower benefits. Benefits for the spouse. Benefits for children. Benefits for survivors. The Social Security reports. Traditional Medicare. Requirements to obtain services. Hospitalization insurance (Part A). Medical insurance (Part B). Drug Insurance (Part D). Medicare Advantage Insurance. Supplemental insurance or Medigap. Medicaid. 1

GOAL 2: PENSION FUND

The importance of a family's pension fund (s). Financial stages. Defined benefit pensions or employer liability. Employee defined contribution pensions. How much must we save to get enough pension? Investment returns. 401k system. IRA system. ROTH system. Practical advice and comments. 15

GOAL 3: EMERGENCY FUND

Emergencies in your working life. Loss of work. Financial responsibilities during the period of unemployment. How much should I save in this fund? The rule of three months. What type of savings and investment accounts you should have? 39

GOAL 4: DO NOT HAVE DEBTS AT THE TIME OF RETIREMENT
Debts during the working period. Why do we get into debt? Good debts and bad debts. How to control debts. Comments on loans. The Credit Report. Credit cards: types, costs and strategies to manage them.......................................43

GOAL 5: HAVE THE HOUSE PAID AND WITHOUT LIABILITIES
The ideal is to get to retirement without the financial and psychological obligation of having to pay a mortgage every month. How to get the mortgage paid by the time of retirement. Cost of maintaining a house during retirement. Rent or own.............................. 73

GOAL 6: RETIRE IN GOOD HEALTH AND ENERGY
This is the most important goal of all the above. The worst thing that can happen to you is to get old without money, being sick or disabled.......................................79

FINANCING CHILDREN'S HIGHER EDUCATION
Families commonly give priority to the education of their children. Costs of education. Capital that is necessary to accumulate to pay these expenses. Commitment with the children. Family savings. Financial assistance from the public and private sector. Educational savings accounts or 529 plans. University prepayment plans. Other forms of financing. How much financial help a student need? Educational savings systems with tax advantages. Federal aid and other types of subsidies. Recommendations. 81

THE INCOME STRATEGY
Keep always in mind what your goals are. Increasing revenue. Income at different ages. Income from employment. Income from a small or micro-enterprise. Factors to improve income.................. 109

THE SPENDING STRATEGY
Keep always in mind what your goals are. Golden rules. Know your expenses well. The psychological factor of shopping. Financial factors of expenditure. What can we do? Basis for an expenditure strategy... 119

THE SAVINGS STRATEGY

Keep always in mind what your goals are. Save for yourself first. Automatic savings. How much savings we need to accumulate to have a decent pension. How to save for the pension fund. Recommendations. 131

THE INVESTMENT STRATEGY

Keep always in mind what your goals are. What is an investment? The risk factors. Risk and diversity. Risk and individual psychology. The long term factors. The compound return factor. The deferred tax factors. Cost of investments. Financial instruments. Ordinary or actively managed mutual funds. Indexed mutual funds. ETF mutual funds. Ordinary versus indexed funds. Why ETF. Investment models.. 139

RECOMMENDED READING

Books, newspapers, magazines, web pages and other media that were consulted and are recommended for a more detailed study of these matters. 169

APPENDIX

SP500 Statistics 173

DEDICATION

In memory of my beloved son Allan L. Garnham

ACKNOWLEDGEMENT

I want to thank my wife Barbara for her editing and proofreading the several drafts of this book and her ongoing support and encouragement during its development.

I also want to thank Juanita M. Dix of J.D. Design for her excellent work designing the cover, formatting the entire document for publication, and providing ongoing advice on publishing.

NOTE TO READERS

FORWORD

This book is written for the middle-income worker of the United States. You will find practical ideas explained in simple language so that you can easily apply them to achieve your financial freedom.

I am convinced that one of the most urgent needs of a person in this century is financial education. The central idea of this book is that anyone can achieve their independence and economic security if they learn to manage their money well. It is a pity that this type of education is not given in most high schools.

The ideas I present in this publication represent my experiences and that of many others I have consulted. Many ideas came as advice from parents to children. Others were practices they had acquired from family and friends. Still others had learned them by observing, studying and reading newspapers and magazines.

What these ideas had in common is that those who applied them became financially independent. Many achieved this status relatively young, which allowed them to engage in other businesses or activities. They learned early on that all the actions they performed had financial impacts or consequences: deciding to study, getting a technical license or achieving a college degree, getting a job, becoming a small business owner, buying a car, buying a house, marrying and having a family, traveling, saving, having a pension fund or investment account, having proper civic behavior, worrying about having good physical and mental health.

Those ideas, thoughts and desires was what kept them focused on activities necessary to achieve their goals honestly and to take advantage of the opportunities offered by the social and economic environment in which they lived. The important thing, they told me, is that they never stopped thinking about becoming financially independent. Moreover, many of them began to feel more secure as they progressed. Seeing that their savings and investments were growing strengthened their efforts to continue to do so.

As you progress in reading this book you will see that economic discipline can also transferred mysteriously to other human activities: a more orderly life, a desire to study and learn more, respect for the law and customs of society, greater appreciation of family life, more participation in community life, better personal presentation, more attention to the spiritual world. It is a spiraling and compound growth: every year the advances that are obtained in some things motivate the advances in others. It is about having more awareness that you can be better, that there is always room to grow in every way, that you can always do things more efficiently.

José Antonio Garnham
Sarasota, Florida
2019

INTRODUCTION AND OVERVIEW

The most intelligent thing that an individual or couple can do is to ensure, as soon as possible, enough capital to generate a minimum income stream to live satisfactorily after a certain age and through old age without worries. In this book my calculations generally are for the financial needs of a couple, with two children – assuming that the two people work and share their income together. The general rule is that the retirement age is about 65 years of age, but we know that some people achieve their economic independence before that milestone, oftentimes during the decade of their 50s years.

The above does not mean that when you achieve your financial independence you must go home and do nothing. On the contrary, what the independence will do is give you peace of mind and the freedom to choose what to do with your life from then on, such as: increasing your minimum income, staying in the workforce, adjusting personal activity, pursuing studies, participating in volunteer work, writing, traveling, becoming further involved with your family, opening up a small business, etc.

Typically, people continue to work until they reach retirement age or beyond if necessary. These people may have achieved their independence much earlier, but decided to continue working for a variety of reasons: satisfaction with work, good salary and benefits, lack of options, inertia, loneliness, etc. Others may be forced to continue working because they started too late to save what is necessary to retire or are saturated with debt.

The problem is to define what is the minimum income you need to feel financially secure and independent. For many, this minimum income from pension funds and social security should be equivalent to 80% of the average annual income of the last three years of ones working life. For others, only 70% of that income might be enough. If the couple has their house paid, has no debt, is in good health, and the children live their independent lives outside the house, that minimum will be easier to reach. In the end, it must be an amount that allows one to live in what one considers an acceptable lifestyle.

No one knows at this point what the future of social security and Medicare programs will be. Most likely, the retirement age will advance to 70 or more years and retirement benefits may be reduced. In turn, similar negative effects could impact Medicare as well. So, it is essential that we embark on creating our own economic security while there is still time.

We are currently living through a substantial change in our economic systems. We live in a global economy, highly technical, in which there is great competition for jobs with good salaries and benefits. It is very possible that the individual of the 21st century will have a very long working life, which will cause him/her to change careers many times either as a professional, technician, small entrepreneur, manual laborer, or administrative worker. This underscores the fundamental principle of having an economic base that gives flexibility to enter and exit the labor market easily.

To do this we must take advantage of financial investment mechanisms. We must not only study them and understand them well, but also be willing to apply them as one more activity in our daily lives. Our retirement funds and other savings will need to be invested in the capital markets (Stock Exchange). This requires us to educate ourselves financially using the information available from financial institutions, books, newspapers, magazines, seminars, conferences, and internet sources.

I have divided this book into two major parts: 1) what are the goals we must achieve for independence and economic security and 2) how can we achieve them. In these parts I discuss in detail the meaning of each goal and the concepts of income, expenditure, saving, and investment.

In summary, the following are important goals:

1. Have Social Security Pension and Medicare Health Insurance.
2. Have pension funds generating income equal to 80% of pre-retirement income.
3. Have a savings and investment account for emergencies and other needs.

4. Have no debts at the time of retirement.

5. Have the mortgage paid and the house cleared of obligations.

6. Have good health at retirement.

As an overview, the first goal is to have contributed to SOCIAL SECURITY AND MEDICARE for the years in which you have worked. This system guarantees a certain income, adjusted for inflation, and health insurance at the end of your working life. The contributions to these systems are mandatory, and to have rights to their benefits, a person must have contributed for at least 10 years. This income is an important supplement to the income you will receive in your pension fund.

Unfortunately for many, social security is the only income they receive when they retire. What is clear from experience is that this income alone is not enough to be able to retire satisfactorily. It was always assumed that social security could represent no more than 40% of the retirement income. For example, in 2018 the average monthly social security pension was $1,400 or $16,800 per year. In this book, we will refer to the family economy, which would equal two incomes for a total annual average income of $33,600 from social security.

As a reference, consider that the federal poverty line[2] for a household of two adults is $16,460 and for a household of four is $25,100. I expect most people do not want to live in their retirement at a level of income almost at the poverty line.

For that reason, the second goal is to create a PENSION FUND from the first moment you start receiving income. There are at least four factors that explain why it is important to start this fund as soon as possible:

1. **The Maximum Possible Monthly Contribution Factor:** Ideally, you should automatically make the maximum possible monthly contribution, without interruption, in your

2. The Federal poverty level is an income standard that the government uses to determine who (individual or household) qualify for federal subsidies or aid like Medicaid or Children Health Insurance.

respective retirement funds. These type of funds (401k, IRA, ROTH, or similar) establish a maximum contribution limit for the employee, which you should use in full. For their part, the employer can, in some cases, also contribute to these funds up to a certain limit depending on the size of the employee contribution. You should make the most of those employer benefits.

2. **The Time Factor:** The more months you make contributions to your pension fund, the greater your accumulation at the time of retirement, especially because of the factors discussed below. Let's not forget that the year that passes without making contributions to your pension fund is a time that does not come back. One can only recover it by making larger contributions in the future.

3. **The Compound Investment Factor:** Every month in your retirement fund accounts, your contributions, interest, and dividends earned are accumulated. As you are not withdrawing the interest you earn each month and you do not withdraw the dividends you receive every three months, these funds earned (together with the new contribution of each month) grow more quickly because each month the base or accumulated capital is bigger.

4. **The Deferred Tax Factor:** In these accounts, income taxes are not paid until you start withdrawing funds, usually after you are 59 ½ years old. Those taxes not paid at that moment, will be invested and earn interest, dividends, and capital gains for years in your retirement fund. This advantage is important because if you do not pay taxes every year, what you earn in your retirement funds will accumulate in a compound way until you start withdrawing funds.

The combined effect of all these factors makes your capital have a much larger and faster accumulation. In addition, note that a small difference in the interest rate or in the number of years invested also makes a big difference in the total accumulation of capital.

For example, a couple who has a gross annual income of $100,000 and contributes to their deferred income pension funds $833 per month ($10,000 per year) or 10% of their gross monthly income for 30 years, invested at a rate of return equivalent to 6% (4% return on investment, plus 2% inflation) will have accumulated a capital of $790,582 dollars at the end of that period. If the rate is 7%, the accumulation will be $944,608. If they save 40 years at the rate of 6%, they will accumulate $1,547,620. If they do so at 7%, they will accumulate $1,966,351.

Imagine how much could be accumulated in our retirement funds if we saved 15% or 20%. These are the secrets of those who become rich: having a smart savings and investing strategy.

The third goal to achieve while you are working is to build a PERSONAL SAVING AND INVESTMENT fund with at least three months of gross salary. While you work and are receiving income, do not forget to deposit into this fund, even if it is a small amount every month. This will give you peace of mind in times of uncertainty when you are in a situation of unemployment, changing work, or training to qualify for a better position. It will also help you cover living expenses during emergencies caused by accidents, natural disasters, damage to your house, car, or other unanticipated event.

A fourth goal is to RETIRE WITHOUT DEBT. During the first years of one's working life when one is starting a family and later during the schooling period of the children, it is reasonable to use loans to cover important expenses.

As time passes it is ideal for the couple to begin paying their debts at an accelerated rate specially when the children are financially independent and outside the home, income is growing and expenses are diminishing. Reaching retirement without debt is an ideal situation which adds to the sense of economic freedom that is so psychologically important when one decides to retire.

Goal number five is to have the HOUSE PAID at the time of retirement or earlier. Ideally, you should do it as soon as possible (refinance for 15 years or less). This can be done by allocating income from salary increases (promotions, bonuses), an inheritance, or a second job dedicated to this purpose. Once the mortgage has been paid in advance, the income released can be deposited in your pension and emergency funds.

Goal six is to retire in GOOD HEALTH. The day you decide to stop working and live from the returns of your investments you will see that having good health to enjoy it is perhaps the most important goal. This is a goal that must be an ongoing focus. We all know what we must do: live without vices, maintain a reasonable weight, exercise, and avoid chronic diseases.

The key here is to consider that the combined effect of all these goals is much larger than the effects of each in isolation (financial synergies).

As a final and separate goal, where children are envisioned, I examine strategies to finance higher education for the children. This issue becomes another financial goal since the education of children is an important priority for a couple.

Unfortunately, not all couples have enough income to create a special fund for education and cannot take advantage of all the taxes and other advantages offered by the different states and the federal government. But those who can do it could benefit from the ideas and information presented here.

Included in this section are ideas for obtaining financing directly from the public and private sectors in the form of scholarships, subsidies, exceptions, donations, or special work programs. Our society is generally very supportive of those, especially with limited means, who strive to get more education and training. This means that students who show ability and commitment may have opportunities for assistance funding their university studies. It helps if there is complementary financing from the family and some income that the student can contribute through his/her own work.

We cannot fail to recognize that higher education of children is one of the most important goals and expenses of low- and middle-income families during their working lives (when they are earning income). Most parents expect their children to go to a university, community college or technical school to learn a profession, or technical or trade skills that will allow them to fend for themselves when they are adults. We all recognize that the best inheritance that can be left to children is a good education and training. This is the motivation behind the higher education funding chapter.

As for how to achieve all of these goals, I have resorted to the old economic formula that says a family income ultimately goes to consumption expenses and for saving through investments.

Income = Consumption Expenses + Savings/Investments

The central point here is that an individual's income is used to finance the normal living expenses of the person or family, and what is left is used for savings and investing in the capital markets (Stock Exchange). Naturally, the fewer expenses, the larger will be the savings and investments. We will explore these concepts in more detail in the chapters that follow.

Normally income increases during the working life of an individual, through salary increases, promotions, bonuses, second jobs, and more benefits. If a person improves his/her knowledge and skills through studies, training, and working experience he/she will see income and opportunities increase. An average person could increase his/her income by moving up in the labor market, applying for better jobs, and finding positions that better match his/her vocation and personal interests. There are always possibilities for improvement. Taking advantage of those possibilities depends in large part on our ability, attitude, and persistence to look for opportunities.

Reducing expenses is another way to have more income for savings. In most cases, family consumption expenses take about 80% of the income of a couple. They include the rent or mortgage of a house, the expenses of public utilities, food, clothes, entertainment, transportation, education, health, etc.

These expenses are difficult to control in the consumer-pressured environment in which most people currently live. Credit cards, personal loans, loans for the purchase of vehicles, student loans, and other offerings influence the spending decisions of individuals. This ease of obtaining a loan has meant that in many cases individuals spend more than is prudent, leaving only a minimum amount for savings or in the worst case leaving nothing for savings.

Savings usually represents what remains after expenses, which ideally may fluctuate around 20% of the income. On average, savings includes the payment of labor taxes for social security and Medicare (7.65%), contributions to pension funds, and other savings such as those for emergencies.

IMPORTANT: A great strategy to save more, is to decide to save first the most you can of your monthly income and spend what is left. This forces the individual or family to limit their expenses to what is available after contributing to the pension and emergency funds. It helps to build discipline for careful spending and avoid negligence or forgetfulness at the moment of saving and investing.

Traditional retirement funds, which are the employer responsibility, have been replaced by retirement funds whose responsibility to contribute, invest, and manage the employee savings rests entirely with employees (401k, IRA, ROTH, etc.). These funds must be invested now under the employee's supervision with the goal that they increase in compound form during the long period of his/her working life, about 40 years. The chapter on investment strategy develops this topic thoroughly and is worth a careful read and study.

Overall this book seeks to stimulate and educate middle-income workers in basic elements of family and personal finance. Its goal is to help individuals and couples achieve a better understanding, control, and decision making regarding their income, expenses, savings, and investments.

Finally, it is important to stress that couples or individuals should consider getting advice on specific questions and situations from financial planners, accountants, or officials of financial institutions where they have opened their accounts or retirement funds. This book gives you basic knowledge about principles and guidance on personal finance to relate effectively with these specialists and form your question and aspirations in order to achieve the goals outlined above.

— GOAL 1 —
SOCIAL SECURITY, MEDICARE AND MEDICAID[3]

Social Security

The Social Security system (SS) is a set of social services established by law to benefit American citizens who meet its requirement. These benefits are financed by contributions to the Social Security funds from the employees and employers.[4]

The Social Security Administration has an excellent website both in English and in Spanish. With your social security number, you can see the details of your account: how much savings you have accumulated, your social security status (how many credits or quarters you have to date); or request a replacement of your social security card and obtain other documents and information.

Since its creation the social security pensions were intended to replace no more than 40% of your preretirement income. It was considered only as a complement to individual pension funds (401k, IRA, ROTH and other similar deferred tax funds) or those created by the companies where you work or just by yourself.

The calculations below show how important it is for a couple to have a Social Security pension. This is monthly income for life, secure

3. The Older American Act was established in 1965 alongside the Medicare and Medicaid Acts. It is a safety net for people over 65 years old that live independent lives.

4. The social security system has a wide variety of benefits and requirements that are not always easy to understand. I recommend getting advice from staff of the Social Security Administration office in your county or city. In this chapter we only present basic information about this system.

and adjusted for inflation annually. It decreases the amount of capital you need in your other pension funds to reach the income that you will need during retirement.

	INCOME THAT PENSION FUNDS SHOULD GENERATE ANNUAL FIGURES FOR TWO PERSON					
DESCRIPTION						
Average gross salary for the last three years	$ 50,000	$ 60,000	$ 70,000	$ 80,000	$ 90,000	$ 100,000
Amount needed to live at 80 % income	$ 40,000	$ 48,000	$ 56,000	$ 64,000	$ 72,000	$ 80,000
Social Security income	$ 20,604	$ 24,180	$ 29,616	$ 31,920	$ 33,600	$ 37,200
Income needed from pension funds	**$ 19,396**	**$ 23,820**	**$ 26,384**	**$ 32,080**	**$ 38,400**	**$ 42,800**

Income from social security is becoming increasingly important in our society. Available official statistics show that for low-income retirees the social security payment represent a little more than 60% of the total income they made before retirement. For middle-income retirees it represents 40% and for high-income retirees 26%. Unfortunately, there is still an increasing percentage of retirees who have only the income from social security to live on once they retire.

To illustrate, in 2018 the average pension paid by social security was $1,404 per month or $16,848 per year or the equivalent of 27.8% of the average (median) annual salary of a working person, which in 2017 was $60,633. See in the table above the calculation you should do if you want to retire today.

The Social Security System of the United States provides the following benefits:

1. Annual pension adjusted for inflation.

2. Disability benefits.

3. Family benefits for the spouse and children.

4. Benefits for survivors: spouse and children.

5. Supplementary income from social security.

6. Health insurance: MEDICARE and MEDICAID

The Pension Fund program is the best known of the Federal Social Security benefits. Each time you receive a salary, this already comes with the mandatory tax deduction for Social Security (benefits 1 to 4) and Medicare (item 6). These two deductions are known as Social Security Tax (FICA – Federal Income Contribution Act). These funds are financed primarily with employee and employer contributions.

The MEDICAID programs and supplemental social security income (benefits 5 and 6) are funded by federal taxes only.

The individual taxes paid to finance your social security are 6.2% calculated on gross salaries up to a maximum of $132,900 (as of 2019). If you earn $150,000 you pay 6.2% on $132,900 only. The taxes paid for MEDICARE are 1.45% of your gross salary, without limit. If you earn $150,000 you pay 1.45% on $150,000. If your annual gross wages are $100,000, $132,900 or $150,000, here are the calculations showing the contributions:

	Contribution %	EMPLOYEE CONTRIBUTIONS ACCORDING TO ANNUAL INCOME							
		SOCIAL SECURITY							
Annual income		$ 50,000	$ 60,000	$70,000	$ 80,000	$ 90,000	$ 100,000	$132,900	$ 150,000
Employee	6.20	$ 3,100	$ 3,720	$ 4,340	$ 4,960	$ 5,580	$ 6,200	**$ 8,240**	**$ 8,240**
Employer	6.20	$ 3,100	$ 3,720	$ 4,340	$ 4,960	$ 5,580	$ 6,200	**$ 8,240**	**$ 8,240**
TOTAL	12.40	$ 6,200	$ 7,440	$ 8,680	$ 9,920	$ 11,160	$ 12,400	$ 16,480	$ 16,480
		MEDICARE							
Employee	1.45	$ 725	$ 870	$ 1,015	$ 1,160	$ 1,305	$ 1,450	$ 1,927	$ 2,175
Employer	1.45	$ 725	$ 870	$ 1,015	$ 1,160	$ 1,305	$ 1,450	$ 1,927	$ 2,175
TOTAL	2.90	$ 1,450	$ 1,740	$ 2,030	$ 2,320	$ 2,610	$ 2,900	$ 3,854	$ 4,350

IMPORTANT: When you start making contributions to social security the system opens an account in your name with your social security number. This means that every month you contribute 6.20% of your gross income to your social security account. Your employer also contributes 6.20% which makes a total monthly contribution to your account of 12.40%. For its part, the employee contribution to Medicare of 1.45% is also doubled with the contribution of the employer for a total of 2.9%. In total, the contribution made to your account by the employer and the employee is 15.3% calculated on your gross income.

In the example above, if you receive wages of $100,000 your account will receive $6,200 each year for social security and $1,450 for Medicare for a total of $7,650 of your contribution and additionally $7,650 of employer contribution for an annual total of $15,300. The contribution to the Social Security Fund is invested to obtain a variable return. After adding inflation, your return is credited to your account.

However, if you are a self-employed worker, your contribution to social security will be 12.40% and Medicare 2.9% for a total of $15,300. This is because you are the employer and employee at the same time.

Time and contribution requirements. To receive benefits from Social Security you must have contributed to social security for at least 10 years or 40 quarters through the course of your working life.

In addition, to receive a quarter of recognition in the system (each quarter is equal to one credit) you must have earned income of at least $1,360 in 2019 and have paid social security taxes. For example, if you had received income in 2019 of $5440 ($ 1360 x 4 quarters) you would be recognized for four quarters or four credits. You cannot receive credits for more than four quarters a year whatever your income. If you are self-employed you must have had net earnings in 2019 of at least $400 to earn a credit or quarter in your account or $1,600 to earn 4 quarters or four credits.

To receive a social security pension, you must meet the age requirements. The calculations of what you can receive according to your age are complicated. We recommend going to the local Social Security office and asking about your situation. As a general guide, here are some basic rules as of 2018:

- 65 and months: if you were born between 1938 and 1943 you can retire at 65 and some months depending on the exact year you were born: 65 years and 2, 4, 6, 8 or 10 additional months.

- 66 YEARS: if you were born between the years 1943-54 you can retire with full pension at 66 years.

- 67 YEARS: if you were born after 1954 you can retire with full pension at 67 years old.

- 62 YEARS: you can retire at age 62, but with a lower pension than what would correspond to the year you were born. This pension is calculated according to the number of months you retire in advance of the age that you would retire with full pension. For each month in advance your pension is reduced by 0.555%.

- For example: if you could retire at age 65 with full pension and decide to retire at age 62, the pension you could have received at age 65 is reduced by 36 months (3 years) multiplied by 0.555% monthly a total percentage reduction of 20%. This 20% reduction is permanent. In other words, your pension for the rest of your life will be the pension you could have received at age 65 but reduced by 20%, plus inflation.

- As you increase the months between the age of 62 and the one that would correspond to the full pension you could receive according to your age, you would receive much less. For example, if you decide to retire at age 62 when you could retire at full pension, age 66, your pension would be 25% less. If you could retire at age 67 but decide to do so at age 62 your pension will be reduced by 30%.

- 65 to 70: you have the option to retire after the official retirement date with full pension. If you postpone your retirement your full pension is increased by a certain percentage until you turn 70, which is retirement deadline. It is worth retiring at age 70 because the difference in value of the pension between age 65 and 70 is very large: 41%.

The social security pension is adjustable according to the consumer price index. This is an important benefit that will accompany you for the rest of your life. It not only adjusts your pension but also all the other benefits of the system. In theory, your pension is adjusted each year according to the inflation of that year.

There is an initiative to change the consumer price index for another one called "chained consumer price index" which is slightly lower than the ordinary consumer price index. Even though there is a small difference between the two, over the years this decreasing affects your income at a time when you can no longer work. An important organization for seniors called the American Association of Retired Persons (AARP), is campaigning to prevent this initiative from being approved.

Benefits for the spouse. The spouse of a beneficiary with full insurance is entitled to receive a pension which varies according to the condition of the beneficiary:

- If the beneficiary receives a full social security pension: the spouse can receive a pension equivalent to 50% of the beneficiary pension if he/she has reached 65 years of age or 40% if he/she has reached 62 years of age. If the spouse has been married for more than 10 years and then has divorced and has not remarried, he/she has the same rights.

- If the beneficiary receives a disability pension: the spouse can receive a pension equivalent to 50% of the beneficiary's pension if the spouse has reached 65 years of age and 40% if he/she has reached 62 years of age.

- If the beneficiary has died: the spouse is entitled to a widow's/widowers pension equivalent to 100% of the beneficiary's pension if the spouse has reached 65 years of age. If he/she is 62 years it is 83% and if 60, 71.5%. There are benefits available for a divorced spouse if he or she has remarried after age 60.

Benefits for children. The children of a beneficiary with full social security insurance are entitled to receive a pension which varies according to the condition of the beneficiary:

- The beneficiary receives a full social security pension: children who are dependent and single under the age of 18 (or younger than 19 but full-time students in a primary or secondary school) are entitled to receive a pension equivalent to 50% from that of the beneficiary. The spouse, of any age, with a child under the age of 16 is entitled to a pension of 50% of that of the beneficiary.

- The beneficiary receives a disability pension: dependent children and unmarried children under the age of 18 (or under 19 but full-time students in a primary or secondary school), can receive a pension equivalent to 50% of the beneficiaries. The spouse of any age with a child under 16 years of age is entitled to a 50% pension.

- The beneficiary has died: unmarried children and dependents under the age of 18 (or under 19 but studying full-time) are entitled to a pension of 75% of that of the beneficiary. The spouse of any age with a child under 16 can receive a 75% pension.

- Children with disabilities have special treatment.

- The parents of the beneficiary who has died are entitled to a pension.

- The spouse who is disabled is entitled to a widower's pension after the age of 50.

Social Security reports. If you do not have an account with the Social Security Administration on the internet, this report is received annually by regular mail. For those who have an internet account in the Social Security Administration the report can be seen on the screen at any time. This report is very important for taxpayers because it contains valuable information about the following:

- An estimate of the amount of pension that you would receive upon meeting the retirement ages and other benefits such as work disability and widowhood pensions.

- A list of all the wages and salaries that the taxpayer has received during his/her working life, as it has been declared to the Social Security Administration. This information should be reviewed by the taxpayer to verify that this list is complete, and its figures correct. If there were errors these could affect the time to meet the minimum required by law to be entitled to social security benefits as well as the number or amount of dollars that should be paid in the form of benefits.

- A list of labor taxes (contributions to social security funds and contributions to MEDICARE) that have been paid by both the taxpayer and the employer.

- If you are already retired and receiving benefits, your account allows you to access a variety of reports and services that you may need from time to time.

It is also important to keep in mind that the social security fund is under permanent review by Congress, the Executive and countless institutions that in one way or another have an interest in this fund. It is recognized that this fund is not a gift that the government makes when you reach retirement age or suffer some disability, but a right that you have based on the contributions that you and your employer made during your working life.

Unfortunately, this fund will probably have a deficit, according to calculations made by various institutions, in about 20 years. The solutions that have been proposed are to increase labor taxes or reduce benefits (including extending the retirement date) or a mixture of both. Most likely, this will affect new retirees in the future, but one must be alert to this issue because it is difficult to know how this problem will be finally be solved. There are a variety of institutions trying to influence the authorities to find a just solution to help support the fund financially.

TRADITIONAL MEDICARE

The information I provide in this chapter is of a general nature. Its purpose is to appreciate the importance of this program for you and your family. Medicare produces a manual in Spanish that you can obtain through the internet or request by phone (1-800-633-4227) to be sent by regular mail.

I recommend that at least 7 months before you turn 65 you go to the local Social Security Service office to speak with an official to learn in detail the procedure to obtain the benefits offered by this system.

It is important that you know there is a limited period each year to register with Medicare. The period to register is from January 1 until March 31. If you do not enroll in that period, you can lose that year and have a penalty which will increase your monthly payment or premium forever. Check with the local Social Security office or the internet about this date.

This is an important benefit that you receive for the rest of your life. You must pay a monthly sum to obtain these services. If you receive Social Security (pension) income the monthly payment to Medicare can be deducted from your monthly social security check.

When you turn 65 you will appreciate that medical services have increased considerably in price. If you have chronic diseases such as diabetes, heart problems, or other ongoing diseases these expenses will go up heavily. Frequent visits to doctors and specialists, medical examinations, prescription drugs, and special treatments increase as the years go by. The basic requirements for obtaining Medicare services are:

- Be a citizen or resident

- Be 65 years old

- Register at the Social Security office. If you are 65 years old and receiving a Social Security pension, you will automatically be registered in Medicare.

- Pay a monthly premium

Medicare has four parts or sections that you must know thoroughly. Again, I recommend that you read the Medicare manual and consult directly with officials of this service, especially if you require hospitalization.

Hospitalization insurance (Part A). It covers expenses for hospitalization, rehabilitation, hospice, and others cost related to hospital care, including ambulances. If you have paid your social security and Medicare taxes during your working life this service is FREE. Otherwise you can buy this service (citizen, resident, 65 years) but it will cost you $441 per month (as of 2018)

Medical insurance (Part B). It covers expenses for services provided by physicians and specialists, laboratory tests, wheelchairs and other equipment, ambulances, and other services that have been determined as necessary by Medicare. In general, this part of Medicare includes the expenses related to medical services designed to prevent you from getting sick (preventive). This program pays 80% of the cost of medical services. The manual indicates all the exams and services of preventive and curative medicine that this part covers. Most insured individuals paid $109 in 2019 for their monthly Medicare premium and this is automatically deducted from one's monthly social security check.

IMPORTANT: The following are services that Medicare does NOT cover:

- Long-term care services

- Routine dental services

- Routine ophthalmological services (eyes)
- Dentures
- Cosmetic surgery
- Acupuncture
- Hearing aids

(Part D) This is a service administered by private companies authorized by Medicare. It covers an important part of the costs of *prescriptions and other medicines* that have been prescribed by doctors. This system is designed to keep the costs of prescriptions low.

Special Insurance (Part C) This part of the Medicare insurance is called MEDICARE ADVANTAGE. It is basically an insurance administered by private companies authorized by MEDICARE to cover the services mentioned in A, B and D. It includes some additional benefits and services if you pay extra for them in the monthly premium of this insurance. MEDICARE ADVANTAGE does not work with MEDIGAP (see below)

The federal government pays the insurance company that participates in this system a certain amount for each person who enrolls in this type of insurance. The insurance company then pays doctors, laboratories, medical centers and hospitals what corresponds to prices previously negotiated. The difference between what the government pays for each enrollee and the services paid by the insurance company are its profits.

COMPLEMENTARY MEDICAL INSURANCE or MEDIGAP

This is insurance sold by private companies. Essentially it is a complementary and optional insurance to the traditional MEDICARE insurance that was created to cover expenses that must be paid directly by the beneficiary (20%) of the part B services. Some MEDIGAP insurance includes pharmacy expenses.

In other words, MEDIGAP helps pay expenses that are not paid by MEDICARE such as: a) deductibles: expenses that must be covered by the insured directly before the insurance begins to pay, b) co-payments: when the cost of a medical service is covered in part by you and part by your insurance and c) co-insurances: payments that are covered by two or more insurances. Some additional rules include:

- You cannot have MEDIGAP insurance that includes pharmacy expenses and MEDICARE Part D at the same time.

- Some MEDIGAP insurances can also pay for medical services when you travel abroad.

- MEDIGAP does not cover dental, optical, eyeglasses, hearing aids, private nursing services, and long-term medical care for the disabled or elderly.

MEDICAID

This is a government social insurance program for people of all ages whose income and assets are insufficient to pay for health expenses.

The system is financed by the federal government, by about 50% of the States (voluntarily) and in some cases the Counties. The federal government establishes the objectives, regulations and programs but the States establish the details of how those regulations will be applied in their territory. In this way, MEDICAID is similar in each state, but not identical.

To be a beneficiary of this system you must be a citizen of the United States or a permanent resident.

Poverty level: an individual's income cannot exceed 133% of the poverty level. The poverty level, in 2018, was $12,140 which means that the income of an individual to be eligible for Medicaid services cannot exceed $16,146 per year.

Type or category of beneficiary: these categories of beneficiaries may vary depending on the state in which they reside. The beneficiaries who can access these benefits can be the following:

- Any low-income beneficiary (less than $16,146 in 2019). This is a voluntary rule for states.

- A group of states do not participate in this new provision, but they maintain the participation requirements that existed before this norm, such as the ones mentioned below:

- Persons over 65 years of low income.

- Pregnant women.

- Children under a certain age of low income.

- Parents of children eligible for Medicaid who meet the income requirements.

- Persons with disabilities who meet certain special Medicaid requirements.

- Persons included in the Supplementary Income Insurance.

Medicaid provides more comprehensive medical services than Medicare. Some people can be covered by MEDICAID AND MEDICARE at the same time, if they meet certain requirements. The services provided by MEDICAID are:

- Medical services like those provided by Medicare and dental services.

- Nursing Special Services for certain beneficiaries. The expenses of this service are first covered with resources of the beneficiary until he/she has spent all of them, then the expenses are covered by MEDICAID.

It is important, if in this situation, that you go to the social services of your state and county to get advice in relation to the benefits you can get given your condition. These services have many details and requirements that are difficult to explain, they also change regularly. It is possible that you can get more benefits than you had expected.

SUPPLEMENTARY SECURTY INSURANCE. - SSI

SSI is cash aid for seniors, specially the blind and disabled, who have very low income even if they have some resources. Even when a person receives income from a job, they may be able to benefit from this program.

To obtain this benefit, a person or relative must apply and meet the following requirements: be a citizen of the United States and a resident of one of the 50 States, the District of Columbia or the Mariana Islands. There are other requirements in relation to persons or families related to the Armed Forces and those who have a criminal past.

In 2019 this SSI grant was $771/month for an individual and $1,157/month for a couple. These subsidies are increased each year with the same percentage that is used to adjust Social Security retirement benefits. In addition, these sums can be reduced in accordance with certain rules regarding other monthly income and property that the beneficiary may have.

This is a complicated issue to understand and if for some reason you are in this situation you should go to the Social Security department in charge of this benefit.

— GOAL 2 —
PENSION FUND

Having a pension fund, in addition to Social Security, is the most important financial goal that every low and middle-income worker should have. Pension funds are financial and legal mechanisms that allow you to accumulate capital from wages, salaries or profits from small businesses. The goal is to grow enough capital to generate a monthly income stream that allows you to live in dignity when you retire. That is the moment when you become financial independent.

Keep in mind that in the last 15 years workers received income from salaries and wages that increased at a rate of about 2.5 % a year. For their part, the investors have been receiving income from interest, dividends, and capital gains at an annual rate of return of about 10% a year. No question the latter is the most effective mechanism to create wealth, income and opportunities and it is for all available only if you know how to use it.

The US pension systems (401K, IRA, ROTH and other similar funds) are the mechanism that allow workers to become investors and get a return similar to that mentioned above. The goal therefore is to transfer to a pension fund all the income possible so you can make it grow at higher rates, in other words, let the capital work for you while your income from labor most probably will remain growing at 2.5% for the foreseeable future.

Increasing your salaries by advancing in your career, continuing to study and train, and getting a second job can help increase your capacity to invest. Having a higher rate of saving, adopting a frugal way of spending and eliminating debt are the tools that you can use to accelerate your accumulation of capital and benefit of the combine effect of compounding, long term investment and deferred taxes that pension funds allow.

In several of my readings about the issue of becoming economically free I realize that the younger workers have at last discovered the benefit of investing through pension funds so they can benefit from compounded returns for a long period of time, without paying taxes until they retire at 59 and a half years old or later. Even more, they learned to invest excess savings outside the pension system but getting the same benefits of a pension fund except deferred taxes and knowing that capital gains taxes are due only when they sell stock.

These young worker-investors created a movement that went viral in the internet and social media that was call FIRE for financial independence retire earlier. Their motto is work to invest and live frugally. They focus on increasing their capacity to generate income (innovation, creativity, studies, training, networking, associating, second job, job changing, small businesses, etc.) and living frugally: smaller houses, low cost clothes and food, eliminating waste, living in groups, sharing, etc.

Maybe this is one of the mechanisms to reduce inequality. The coming of a new high technology revolution is going to change the world of labor and require new labor policies will need to be implemented in order to create new opportunities for workers to obtain jobs with higher income. Until then, workers will have to use everything that is available to increase their knowledge and skills, gain experience, form attitudes and learn to take advantage of what is available for them.

There are several other reasons WHY you should open an account in a tax deferred pension fund:

1. The new regulations for retirement funds require active participation of the employee to make the maximum possible contribution for the longest period of time, invest those savings wisely and follow-up its returns. You should learn how to do this.

2. The sooner you open this pension account during your working life the longer the time of accumulation you will have.

3. The contribution of employers to pension funds has decreased while the life of retirees has lengthened. Only 40% of the employees of corporations with less than 100 employees are covered by employer's pension plans.

4. Unfortunately, not all employees have saved enough in their pension funds to be able to retire comfortably: it is estimated that less than 65% of employees have done so.

5. Most employees and small business owners have great confidence that when they retire their financial problems will be solved.

6. Part of the problem is that many do not know how much it will cost to live during retirement. They cannot imagine the strong impact that inflation and a longer life will have on their finances.

7. Many blindly save without knowing how much they will need to accumulate to generate enough income during the years of retirement. They usually save much less than they should and miss many opportunities to benefit from the advantages offered by pension systems. They do not worry about the vagaries of the stock market because they simply do not have investments.

8. On the other hand, many think that they will continue to work for income until the end of their lives, something very risky as old age approaches and job opportunities decrease when skills become obsolete, one has less energy and possible health problems. Statistics show that only about 30 to 35% can continue working.

9. Nor do many consider that social security income during retirement will be insufficient to maintain a reasonable lifestyle as members of the social class to which they belong. Even more, many do not know how much they will receive when they retire.

This is the result of the avalanche of new retirees (baby-boomers) that began their retirement years in 2012 (10,000 are incorporated every day into the social security system). In addition there are the effects the economic crisis of 2007-09; of the future fiscal deficits and the enormous public debt that has accumulated. Only recently, alternatives are being publicly discussed to save the social security that is expected to run out of funds by the mid-2030s.

These alternatives include extending the retirement age progressively until age 70, reducing payments, either by freezing or adjusting downward, increasing the tax contributions to the fund, among others. All this will affect the income of those who retire in the next 15 to 20 years.

It is important to consider that for about 50% of those who are retired, social security income represents the most important income they have for living. Despite this, many do not realize the importance of social security benefits and the need to defend this program. Do not forget that among its benefits are payment of an (adjusted for inflation) old age life pension, payments for physical or mental disability and payments for the survival of a spouse.

Similarly, if the social security fund is depleted, Medicare benefits may be diminished, and insurance premium payments increased. Medicare is an important benefit for the finances of the family or an individual. This is a benefit that few understand and value during their working lives. Similarly, employers of small businesses do not know much about existing pension funds for employers and employees. These funds are inexpensive and can substantially improve the retirement benefits.

In addition, we do not know how long our lives will be after we retire. The figures that actuaries use to calculate life insurance is 100 years for those who now begin their working life around 25 years of age. The number of years that a person may live in retirement could also be longer especially when in good health due to the advances of medicine and better education. This means that your income should also last a longer period.

The combined effect of all the above will mean employees who are planning their retirement must make important decisions. These include decisions to increase their contributions to pension funds, seek more efficient investment mechanisms, generate additional savings, seek a second job, extend the retirement date, continue working during one's retirement years, eliminate debts, renegotiate mortgages or pay them off as soon as possible in order to ensure financial security.

FINANCIAL STAGES IN THE LIFE OF A PERSON

The Development Stage. This period covers the first 25 years of a person's life. It is an important part of one's life and is dependent on what parents do and what we can do ourselves. Nutrition and health during the first years of one's life, quality education until the end of one's high school and university studies, care of one's health and nutrition during adolescence and, above all, formation of character during all these years. The latter includes the package of values, behaviors and customs that will accompany us for the rest of our lives.

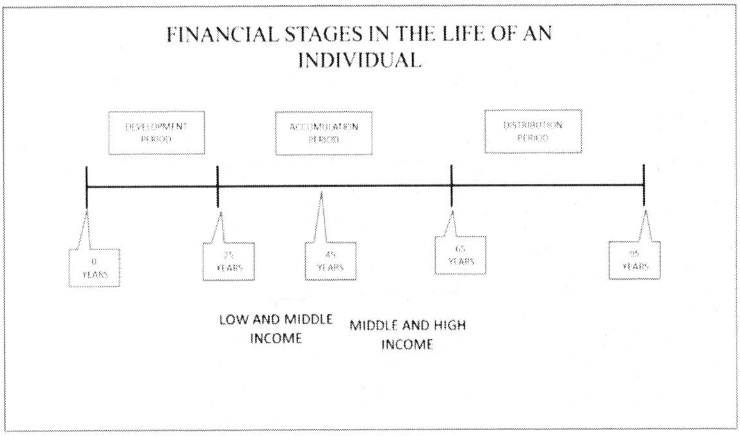

Our first teachings come from our parents who give us their example and discipline. Religion gives us beliefs and values. The example of relatives, friends and teachers complement our education about how to behave in society. All of these are creating our character and a way of being and acting that are imprinted in our minds for the rest of our lives.

This package of values and customs plus the knowledge we acquire studying will be the tools that will allow us to earn a living for ourselves and our family and make valuable contributions to our society. The level of income and progress in work/career as employees, professionals or small entrepreneurs will be in proportion to what we have in that backpack. Our accumulated knowledge, information and character that we receive in this stage will define our economic future unless we win the lottery, receive an inheritance or just have a lot of luck.

The Accumulation Stages. This is the period when you are working as an employee or a small entrepreneur. This period normally covers from 25 years old, when it is assumed that work begins in a stable form, until 65 years old, the date when we assume retirement begins. Statistics show that more than 90% of individuals retire between 62 and 65 years of age.

SOME PRIORITIES DURING OUR RETIREMENT PERIOD

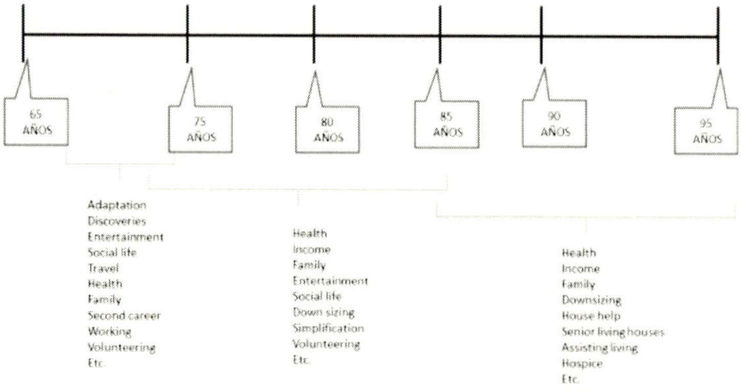

In this period, you accumulate capital (savings and investments) to retire at age 65 or before if you have had the ability to achieve your financial goals at a younger age. Or you retire after that age if you still need to continue working to obtain your financial security or independence.

Remember that your goal is to retire in economic dignity, that is, living comfortably in accordance with the lifestyle you have selected. This means that you must have capital that generates an income equivalent to at least 80% of your pre-retirement expenses or a smaller percentage if you select a more frugal lifestyle or an earlier retirement.

The Distribution Stage. This stage starts when you leave work. Today, life expectancy for a person of 65 years is 80 years and will continue to increase with the advances of medicine. It is very possible that for those who begin their working life today, their life expectancy will be 100 years or more, a figure that actuaries are beginning to use as noted earlier. In summary, you should assume for your financial calculations that you will live in retirement at least 20, 30 or more years, depending on your current age.

These life expectations help define how much capital you should accumulate for a flow of income that is enough to live the rest of your life. That should be the period where you can live a high-quality life if you achieve your financial goals: the six goals mentioned at the beginning of this book.

DEFINED BENEFIT FUNDS

Defined benefit funds are those pension systems where responsibility to establish, administer and finance them is entirely with the employer. In almost all cases, the employee participates in some form of financing through monthly contributions automatically made through deductions from salary. This deduction is made according to a formula previously agreed with the employer.

The responsibility to invest those funds and to pay employees' pensions for life is with the employer. Think about the pension systems that existed in the automotive companies (General Motor, Ford and Chrysler). Federal, state, county and municipal government funds had been structured mostly that way, for example, for the police, firemen, administrative employees, professionals.

Over time these defined funds began to be underfunded and companies began to have serious problems to meet their obligations to pay pensions to retirees. Part of the problem was the fact that the companies made low-interest loans against these funds to finance their normal operations and then had difficulties paying them back.

In addition, many companies with financial problems did not deposit enough funds to the pension funds such that debt was gradually increasing to almost unmanageable amounts as employees began collecting pensions. Also, the administration of these pension funds was of poor quality and expensive, which meant low rates of return. These problems happened almost all at the same time, both in the public and private sectors.

In short, this system became increasingly complicated and more expensive for companies. So many decided to pass responsibility for the contribution and management of funds to the employees themselves. Being the direct beneficiaries, they supposedly would be more careful in fund administration. These funds became known as defined contributions.

In the last 20 years, defined benefit pension funds have decreased substantially to be replaced by defined contribution funds. The non-federal public sector has gradually begun to have the same type of transformation.

DEFINED CONTRIBUTION FUNDS.

These are funds where employees make contributions in a special account opened in their name by the employer (401k) or directly by the employee (IRA, ROTH), according to a certain formula that establishes a limit. The employer can make a voluntary contribution to the employee's account also according to a formula. These are deferred taxes accounts.

DESCRIPTION	INCOME THAT PENSION FUNDS SHOULD GENERATE ANNUAL FIGURES FOR TWO PERSON					
Average gross salary for the last three years	$ 50,000	$ 60,000	$ 70,000	$ 80,000	$ 90,000	$ 100,000
Amount needed to live at 80 % income	$ 40,000	$ 48,000	$ 56,000	$ 64,000	$ 72,000	$ 80,000
Social Security income	$ 20,604	$ 24,180	$ 29,616	$ 31,920	$ 33,600	$ 37,200
Income needed from pension funds	**$ 19,396**	**$ 23,820**	**$ 26,384**	**$ 32,080**	**$ 38,400**	**$ 42,800**

The important thing to emphasize in this type of account is that it is the *employee* who has the responsibility to invest his/her savings in the pension fund. Hence the importance for an employee or small entrepreneur to educate themselves about personal finance because they will have many decisions to make and follow-up in the future.

In a deferred tax account, employee contributions and those made by employers do not pay income taxes until they retire and meet the legal requirements to begin withdrawing funds. The interest, dividends and capital gains also do not require payment of taxes annually, but only at the time of withdrawal.

HOW MUCH SHOULD I SAVE IN MY PENSION FUND TO RETIRE IN DIGNITY?

If you retired today, are in the gross income category of $100,000, you would need to have accumulated in your pension funds a capital of $856,000 to generate $42,800 per year. This capital every year should increase 7% (5% return on investment and 2% inflation). If you withdraw every year no more than 5% of the income for your expenses, the funds would continue to grow only because of inflation. At the end of your life you would leave your heirs the same capital with which you started, adjusted by inflation.

But the specific question is how much you should save annually during your working life to raise the $856,000 of capital needed to generate the annual $42,800 mentioned above?

To simplify the answer, I can only tell you that if a couple had saved $10,000 per year ($833 per month) for 30 years, and had invested religiously every month, without skipping any month, with an average annual return of 7%, they would have accumulated a capital of $944,608. If they had done the same for 40 years, the accumulated total would be $1,966,351. This is due to the magic of compound growth, non-payment of taxes during this period and the long period of time during which investments are made. See table above on page 23 for other options.

	ANNUAL RETURNS OF INVESTED FUNDS				
ANNUAL INCOME	ANNUAL SAVING 10%	RETURNS 6% 30 YEARS	RETURNS 7% 30 YEARS	RETURNS 6% 40 YEARS	RETURNS 7% 40 YEARS
$ 50,000	$ 5,000	$ 395,290	$ 472,304	$ 773,810	$ 998,176
$ 60,000	$ 6,000	$ 474,349	$ 566,765	$ 928,572	$ 1,197,811
$ 70,000	$ 7,000	$ 553,407	$ 661,226	$ 1,083,334	$ 1,397,446
$ 80,000	$ 8,000	$ 632,465	$ 755,686	$ 1,238,096	$ 1,597,081
$ 90,000	$ 9,000	$ 711,523	$ 850,147	$ 1,392,858	$ 1,797,716
$ 100,000	$ 10,000	$ 790,582	$ 944,608	$ 1,547,620	$ 1,966,351

This analysis suggests you have several options available:

- You could save much more than 10%. Some millennials are now saving up to 50% of their income with the goal of obtaining their financial independence sooner.

- You could determine to spend less during your retirement, say, only an equivalent to 70% of the gross income you received when you were working or you could decide to spend more, for example 110%.

These scenarios mean that you would need to accumulate less or more in your pension fund. You could also determine to leave less capital to your heirs or simply leave them nothing. In this last case, your annual availability of funds would be bigger each year because you would be spending all your capital which would be zero when you die.

In general, estate planning and retirement questions are not easy to answer. Young couples will probably save less during their first 10 to 15 years of working life and then increase that percentage as their income increases over the years because of promotions, experience, additional studies, job market opportunities, etc. At the same time their expenses will be diminished when they have paid off their mortgage and when the children become economically independent.

The US Department of Labor reported as of mid-2017, that the median income in the country was $57,652 for a household. The poverty line in the USA, in 2019, was $25,100 for a family of four. It is considered that double this figure ($50,200) corresponds to a low-income family. At the same time, the average social security pension was $16,416 in 2017.

What should you know about the different pension funds?

- These funds have regulations that are complex, with many turns, exceptions, and classifications that will inevitably force you to consult with your personnel office or specialist to be sure that you have chosen the best system.

- If you are a self-employed worker or small business owner, you should consult with your accountant or a financial institution specializing in these pension systems.

- If you are a person who likes to study these subjects directly you can go to the website of the U.S. Internal Revenue Service where you will find in English and Spanish, the regulations related to all these funds (www.irs.gov). Also, financial institutions in their web pages (Schwab, Fidelity, Vanguard and others), present good information on these matters. Finally, in the last section of this book (Recommending Reading) where several authors are indicated who have analyzed these topics in depth.

In the following paragraphs you can find basic information about these funds to help you understand structure: who can open an account in a pension fund, how much can you contribute annually, how much can your employer contribute, what tax benefits do you have, when can you begin to withdraw funds, which fines exist, how your pension fund can be carried with you when you move from one job to another, etc.

Knowing and understanding this basic information will help you communicate easily with the personnel office or financial institution in which you will open your account or already have an account.

Finally, I must point out that all the regulations of these pension systems have been created to benefit employees, particularly those with lower incomes. They encourage employees to save through pension funds, so that, in the long term, they can raise enough capital to generate income, that when added to social security, allows one to retire in dignity.

TRADITIONAL 401k[5]

These funds are opened by employers for the benefit of their employees. They can be established by corporations, limited corporations, business owners, non-profit organizations (501c3) or government entities. They are administered by employers through financial corporations. The human resources departments give advice on how to register in these plans and how they operate.

BENEFIT FOR EMPLOYEES

The employee can contribute a percentage of his/her total compensation (salary, bonuses, commissions, etc.). This contribution can be made automatically, subject to prior authorization of the employee. It is highly recommended that the employee do this automatically as it facilitates the accumulation of capital without the need for the employee to do anything personally every month. This also helps avoid the problem of oversight or negligence.

The investment of funds that accumulate in these accounts (contributions, interest, dividends, capital gains) is the sole responsibility and control of the employee. They decide what to invest and can change their investments as many times as they wish, within the

5. Other similar funds are 403 (b) retirement plans for specific employees of public schools, tax-exempt organizations and certain ministers; 457 (b) retirement plan available only to state and federal employees or employees of tax-exempt organizations.

regulations of the retirement plan that the employer has contracted. Normally employers, through the financial companies that administer these plans, offer investment instruments such as mutual funds, balanced funds, target-type funds, purchase of shares, bonds, money instruments and other forms of investment. On average these companies offer around 28 funds or investment plans.

The earlier an employee begins to make contributions, the longer the accumulation and investment time will be. A long period of time allows investments to grow larger by effect of compounded growth (such as compounded interest rates).

The contributions, interest, dividends and capital gains that accumulate over the years in these accounts are exempt from tax until when withdrawals are made. This benefit is called deferred tax. An employee can start withdrawing funds from these accounts without paying fines at 59½ years old. From age 70 ½ one is obliged to withdraw annually a sum according to a formula established by the Internal Revenue Service.

If a person withdraws funds from these accounts earlier, they must pay a fine equal to 10% of the amount withdrawn. There are exceptions such as death, permanent physical or mental incapacity, medical expenses and others. If a person does not withdraw the corresponding funds after he reaches 70 ½ years, he must pay a fine of 50% of the amount he should have withdrawn.

Administrative, investment and external consulting expenses are charged against these accounts. Supposedly the 401k funds benefit the employer because administrative expenses are lower than those of "defined benefits" in which the pensions are the employer's full responsibility.

Every year, the Internal Revenue Service establishes the maximum amount an employee can contribute to all 401k accounts, including ROTH 401k accounts. For 2019 that amount is $19,000. If the employee is over 50, he/she could make an additional contribution of $6,000, which means a maximum of $25,000 for 2019.

Employers can contribute voluntarily to the 401k accounts of their employees. Normally employers do so through a matching system based on the total contribution made by the employee. It is common for employers to limit their contribution to no more than 3 to 6% of the employee's income. For example, an employee earns $40,000 and contributes to his/her 401k account equivalent to 5% of his/her total income. The employer offers a contribution equivalent to 50% of the employee's contribution, but with a limit of 3% of his/her income. The employee contributes $2,000 and the employer $1,000 or 2.5% of $40,000 or half (50%) of the employee's contribution for a total of $3,000.

As another example, the employer may decide to contribute equivalent to that made by the employee up to a certain limit. Assume an employee earns $50,000 and decides to contribute 8% of that income to his/her 401k account, the employer offers to contribute 10% of the employee's income up to the amount of the contribution made by the employee. The employee's contribution is $4,000 and the employer's contribution is also $4,000. The latter could have been $5,000 (10%) if the employee had contributed that amount.

If the employee had decided to maximize his/her contribution, he/she would have contributed $19,000 and the employer $5,000, the maximum contribution the employer offered. The employee could have added $6,000 if he/she had been over 50, for a total contribution of $30,000.

When employers contribute to the fund, they are inducing employees to open accounts of this type and make the maximum possible contributions to benefit from the maximum contribution that the employer can make. For their part, employers can deduct their contributions from their taxes.

Employers offer contributions when they want to retain valuable employees for the company.

It is important to note that lately employers are automatically enrolling their employees. They may later opt out of this plan.

Employer contributions and earnings on those contributions are partially owned by the employee according to certain formulas related to the number of years he/has worked at the company.

PROBLEMS RELATED TO THESE ACCOUNTS:

Many employees don't know how to use the benefits offered by these funds. In other words, they have not made enough large contributions but have preferred to spend more and save less or nothing. According to the Wall Street Journal about half of the families with a head of household from 60 to 62 years old have saved less than 25% of what they should or could have saved in their 401k accounts.

Also, entrepreneurs contributed less during the financial crisis that began in September 2007. They were contributing according to the profits they obtained. As their contributions are voluntary, they eliminated, reduced or simply established a fixed contribution amount (for example $500). In general, employers do not want to promise a contribution and then remove it, so they are very cautious about the level at which they start.

Employees also have made many mistakes in the management of these accounts. The way many have organized their investments (corporate shares, bonds, money, market mutual funds, etc.) has been inadequate for their ages and special circumstances or projected needs.

New rules of the U.S. Labor Secretary require that companies with these plans give financial advice to their employees. The most common approach is for companies to hire advisory and administrative services from specialized financial institutions.

Financial advisory companies in turn have presented some problems. Administrative expenses, financial transaction fees and other expenses have been very high in some cases. This has motivated the government to force these financial companies to report in detail all the expenses that they charge to the clients in this system.

Of course, this 401k system has many complexities, conditions and other details that are not easy to understand from reading the manuals. In addition, your company must have financial advisors or qualified personnel in its personnel department who have the obligation to know these matters in depth and explain them when a 401k account is opened.

PRACTICAL TIPS

The first thing to do is to go to your personnel office to find out about the pension plans your company offers. If possible, proceed at that time to register in the 401k plan and set up an automatic deduction from your salary to be deposited in an account opened in your name, along with any employer contribution.

Do not think much about this. Do it with your eyes closed and adjust your expenses to the level of net income you will have after that deduction. This decision will be one of the most important that you will make in your working life. Little by little you will see how that account grows with your contributions and the income you get from investing those deposits.

This type of plan is not easy to understand and assimilate. You should concentrate on doing well what you can, which is: a) with your employer establish a mechanism of monthly savings, as far as possible automatic, and b) invest those funds prudently.

It is very possible that your company will have hired a specialized financial company for managing the 401k plan for its employees. These may include Vanguard, Schwab or Fidelity or other similar financial institutions. Fidelity, for example, manages more than 11 million accounts of this type. These companies offer extensive information to employees who have 401k account with them.

Do not miss the opportunities offered by these companies to financially educate yourself. Go to their seminars, especially with your spouse or partner. Read the information they offer on their web pages or in the printed materials they regularly send you. Talk to the officers. Make yourself known, visit periodically or call by phone. Establish a relationship of trust and for seeking advice.

The bottom line is to make the maximum possible contribution and take advantage of the contribution offered by the employer. Act immediately to maximize the benefit from compounding, long time investing and deferred taxes. The goal: to grow your pension fund faster and bigger.

Another tip is to diversify the investments in this 401k account. If you are a young person, invest in a more aggressive way, but with controlled risk such as buying shares of passive or indexed mutual funds following the SP500 index. See the chapter on investment strategies.

One of the advantages of these 401(k) accounts is that in most cases you can take them with you when you change jobs. You do not lose anything in doing so. What I recommend is that you do not take money out of this account. Simply move it electronically to your new workplace. The personnel office will help you do this. Another way, when there is no possibility of transferring it to another 401k account, is to make a transfer to an IRA account that you can open in any financial institution.

Even if allowed, do not take loans against your 401k. Look for other ways to finance your down payment for a house or a car or to handle an emergency. This fund should be considered sacred to you and you should not touch it or compromise it.

THE SYSTEM 401k - ROTH PLAN

The 401k plan allows employees to transfer all or part of their contributions to a 401k-ROTH account. This contribution is made after the employee has paid taxes on the income of that contribution. It is important to keep in mind that the sum of contributions to the Roth 401k account and the traditional 401k account cannot be higher than $18,000 in 2017. You can add $6,000 for employees over 50 years old.

After 59 and a half years of age, the employee can begin to withdraw funds accumulated in his/her 401k-Roth account (contributions, interest, dividends, capital gains) free of income tax. This is a great benefit, so it is advisable to start contributing to an account of this type when you are young, and your tax rate is low.

Employer contributions are deposited in a separate 401k-ROTH account because they are contributions that have not paid taxes. Employers will pay taxes on the employer's contributions when the employee starts making withdrawals from that contribution. Interest, dividends and capital gains accumulated in this account are not subject to taxes at the time funds are withdrawn. The employee must fulfill a certain number of years in the company to be entitled to these funds and their profits.

It is worth reviewing some of the advantages of the 401k-Roth plan:

- Contributions to a Roth 401k account are not subject to an annual income limit (wages and benefits) as is the case with an ordinary Roth-IRA account.

- The employee can transfer accumulated funds in a Roth 401k account to a Roth-IRA account and avoid being subject to mandatory distributions after 70 ½ years.

- The contribution that can be deposited in a ROTH 401k account is greater than that of an ordinary Roth-IRA account.

The 401k accounts allow the establishment of pension funds for small entrepreneurs and self-employed workers. These are called SIMPLE 401k. Check with financial institutions such as Schwab, Fidelity, Vanguard or a bank where you wish to establish these funds.

IRA – INDIVIDUAL RETIREMENT ACCOUNTS

One of the best-known pension fund systems is the IRA or Individual Retirement Account. This system consists of at least the following types of accounts that you can choose from depending on your situation as an employee, employer, self-employed worker or small business owner.

- Traditional IRA for employees

- ROTH - IRA for employees.

TRADITIONAL IRA

These accounts are established for the exclusive benefit of the ones who open them. They can only be opened in a bank, another financial institution, a credit union that is insured by the government, or any other entity approved by the U.S. Internal Revenue Service (IRS). These institutions are the custodians of your account. It is common for such accounts to be opened with a bank or financial institution such as Fidelity, Schwab, Vanguard or other similar company.

There are a few basic rules:

- IRA accounts can be opened only by citizens and residents who have a salary from an employer or an income from working on their own and who meet the minimum requirements.

- An account can be opened even if you have a retirement plan in the company where you work, in which case your contributions are limited to a certain formula.

- This account can be opened at any time in the calendar year, even until April 15 of the following year (deadline to file the income tax).

- Your contributions must be in cash or check. This rule does not apply if you are transferring funds in electronic form from an IRA or 401k account or other accounts similar to an IRA.

- Deposits can only be made in these accounts up to the maximum limit set for each year: for 2019 that limit was $6,000. If you are over 50, you can add $1,000 which makes a total of $7,000 of maximum limit. If you have more than one IRA, the contributions made to all your IRAs can not exceed the annual limit: $6,000 or $ 7,000, as applicable.

- If you and your wife jointly file tax returns, you can each make separate contributions to your respective IRA accounts for a total of $6,000 ($7,000) each. If one of the spouses (in joint returns) does not have enough income to pays taxes that person is still allowed to make contributions to an IRA up to the limit.

- If a person earns less than the $6000 limit ($7,000), he/she can only make contributions up to the amount earned. If you make contributions above the limit you have to pay a fine equivalent to 6% on the excess. You have until April 15 of each year to withdraw the excesses.

- There is an income limit for a person who wants to make a maximum contribution. In 2019 a single person cannot make contributions to a IRA account if they receive income more than $74,000 and if they are married filing jointly, they cannot not do so if their income exceeds $123,000.

PAYMENT OF TAXES AND FINES

Contributions made to IRAs can be deducted from personal income when calculating the amount of tax to pay on income each year. In this sense, they are deferred tax accounts: you pay taxes on contributions and the profits obtained from your investments only when you start withdrawing funds, which can be done without paying a fine, starting at 59 ½ years.

When a person turns 70 ½ years it is not possible to continue making contributions to his/her IRA. Furthermore, at that age it is mandatory to start making withdrawals (distributions) of a minimum amount calculated according to a formula based on age. You can withdraw a figure greater than the minimum or even the entire balance of your account. But remember that the amounts that you withdraw from your IRA are added to the income on which you must pay taxes that year.

IMPORTANT: there are special rules that state how you can deduct your IRA contribution from your income. If you have a retirement plan in the company where you work this deduction may be limited depending on your total income and your tax status (married filing a joint or separate return or being single or head of household).

SPECIAL SITUATION: *You can participate in a retirement plan in your company and contribute up to the limit to your IRA, but not have the contribution deducted from your taxable income for that year. This situation is very favorable for a person who wants to invest those funds free of annual taxes without paying fines. In this case, your contributions to this type of IRA have already paid the taxes so that you pay taxes only on capital gains, dividends and interest when you start to withdraw at retirement. This means that you must keep separate accounts of the original contribution and investment income.*

Fines for early withdrawal of funds (before 59 ½) are 10%. But there are exceptions to this rule: early death, physical disability, purchase of a home for the first time, college education expenses, etc. Withdrawal of funds after the mandatory (70 ½) pays a 50% fine on the amount not withdrawn.

REMEMBER: THE INVESTMENT OF FUNDS IN AN IRA ACCOUNT ARE EXCLUSIVELY THE RESPONSIBILITY OF THE EMPLOYEE WHO OPENS THE ACCOUNT IN HIS/HER NAME.

There is a wide variety of investment instruments: certificates of deposits, federal, state and municipal bonds, money market accounts, stocks, ordinary mutual funds, indexed mutual funds, Exchange Trade Funds (ETF), etc. However, there are certain investments that are prohibited: options, life insurance and collectibles such as works of art, antiques, precious metals and stones, stamps and coins, alcoholic beverages. There are exceptions: you can buy US gold, silver and platinum coins and bullion from those metals.

You cannot obtain a loan from an IRA, nor can you put it as collateral on a loan. Neither can you sell or rent a property and put the proceeds into an IRA, buy a property with IRA funds for personal use, or receive a high compensation for managing an account of this type.

If you have a retirement fund in one company and you change to another or you become unemployed, you can transfer (rollover) the retirement funds to another IRA account opened for this purpose.

Finally, it is important to consider that IRAs are not protected against claims of creditors. However, some states consider that in case of bankruptcy some protection can be provided when the income from this account is essential for the basic maintenance of the debtor and his/her family.

THE ROTH-IRA SYSTEM

This system is a variation of the IRA system. Both have the same standards and requirements except in the following aspects.

The contributions made to these accounts must first pay income tax. The great advantage is that the contributions and gains from the investment (interests, dividends and capital gains) are not subject to taxes when withdrawn.

A second advantage is that there is no age limit to withdraw funds after one has reached 59 ½ years. Furthermore, a person can continue to make contributions after 70 ½ if they continue to work and generate income.

The limit of contributions that can be made to a ROTH-IRA account is the same as for an IRA: $6,000 in 2019 and an additional $1,000 if you are over 50.

What is different here is the income limit that a person must contribute. In 2019 a single person cannot make contributions to a ROTH account if they receive income more than $122,000 and if they are married filing jointly, they cannot not do so if their income exceeds $193,000

You may have several IRAs and ROTH-IRAs, but the total contributions made to these accounts in one year cannot be more than the $6,000 limit ($7,000).

There are several rules that must be met to ensure that withdrawal of funds from these accounts are free of tax. One of them is that the withdrawals are made after five years of opening the account and that the person is over 59 ½ years old. There are exceptions: if the person is incapacitated or wants to buy a first home. If the owner of the account dies, the funds can be withdrawn by the heirs without paying fines.

The system of IRA accounts includes a simplified system of savings and investment for self-employed and for small entrepreneurs. These pension funds are known by the name SEP-IRA. If the company has less than 100 employees, the employer can establish a pension fund called SIMPLE-IRA.

You can obtain information about these two IRA systems directly from the financial institutions or banks where you wish to establish these funds, such as Schwab, Fidelity, Vanguard or other similar financial institutions.

GOAL 3

EMERGENCY FUND

Ideally every individual or couple should have a savings and investment account in a bank or financial institution to fulfill the objective of accumulating funds for emergencies. These savings are in addition to those in the retirement funds. In this emergency fund an amount equivalent to three or more gross monthly wages should be accumulated.

These savings should cover the basic monthly family expenses as well as the mandatory expenses such as mortgage, car loan, contributions to pension funds and insurance premiums.

The idea is to cover emergency situations that occur during your working life. One of the most important is to meet financial obligations when you lose your job or decide to move to a better one with higher salary and more prospects for advancement. We know that it takes time to find a job again. The preparation of resumes or curricula vitae, filling applications, maintenance of correspondence, carrying out interviews, participation in work connection networks, updating and expansion of knowledge through courses, seminars and specialized training, and several other job-hunting activities take time and consume resources.

Finding a job or moving to a new one has been experienced in dramatic ways by many people since the crisis of 2007-09. Despite having managed to avoid a major crisis and even with improvements in economic and labor conditions in recent years there are still serious challenges such as getting better real wages for low and middle-income workers. In 2019, real wages have had the same purchasing power as they had in 2006.

Other emergencies needing special funds could relate to health problems from accidents or other causes that your health insurance does not cover or covers only partially. Frequently, the insurance is too slow to recover what you have already spent unexpectedly and urgently.

It is also possible that you must assume this type of expense for members of your immediate family such as your parents or siblings. It is important that you analyze these responsibilities well in order not to have surprises that may deplete your savings in a mayor way or oblige you to assume debts beyond your ability. It is important to talk with family members and explain this situation clearly so that everyone takes precautions and avoids as far as possible emergency expenses.

Other emergencies include those arising from accidents that occur to your automobile or work vehicle. Car insurance has a deductible that you must cover. It is common that today we need two vehicles: one to go to work and another for taking children to and from school, to special classes, going shopping, going on vacation, visiting family and friends, etc.

A fund of this type also allows one to raise money to form the "down payment" to buy a house. This goal is very important for couples who are thinking of getting married or are newly married. Even when there are subsidies or special grants for first-time homebuyers, all other financial institutions require no less than 20% as a down payment with high- and steady-income levels.

You can also put money in this emergency account for the "down payment" you need to buy a vehicle. The more you pay in cash the less debt and interest payments you will have. Also, with a high down payment (20 or 30%) you can negotiate a better price and loan rate.

There may be other emergencies that can be covered totally, partially or temporarily with accumulated savings in this fund. Examples could relate to recovering from natural disasters which are becoming more common such as earthquakes, tsunamis, floods, landslides or hurricanes, etc. These have created economic havoc in families from which they are able to recover only after a long time and with great sacrifices.

The theft of your work tools (machinery, equipment, tools, computers, inventories) is another occasion where emergency funds may be needed. Such robberies increase significantly in times of great unemployment. Pawn shops and companies that buy and sell stolen goods including metals have been very active lately according to the police.

Once such emergencies are addressed, this saving and investment account should be replenished as soon as possible, and you should continue saving for the rest of your working life. What you accumulate in this fund is capital, which when well invested will allow you to obtain additional income for your pension funds.

REMEMBER, THESE TYPES OF ACCOUNTS REQUIRE PAYING TAXES ON INTERESTS, DIVIDENDS AND CAPITAL GAINS.

How can we generate savings to deposit in an Emergency Fund?

Today there are several strategies to generate such savings. I would suggest that the most important is automatic savings. Go to the personnel office where you work and ask the person in charge to deduct a certain percentage (3%?) of your salary every month and deposit it in your savings and investment account as an emergency fund. As the years go by, you can increase your contributions to this account when salaries are higher due to seniority and promotions.

Just close your eyes and make that move. Your liquid salary, which is given to you in a check at the end of the month will be less. But this will force you to adapt to that level of income. But you will do it knowing that you are capitalizing part of your income. Undoubtedly, you will have to live more modestly, but that is the challenge. For sure you can do it. You are smart.

REMEMBER: WORK FOR INVESTING NOT FOR EXPENDING

You must be very careful not to compromise these savings with increases in your credit card expenses, as that destroys the whole purpose of saving for this fund.

It is good to live modestly, sharpen the senses, and become more creative in the selection of the things you buy. This approach allows you to live frugally. You will feel more efficient, safe, comfortable and satisfied when you are saving more and spending wisely.

It is important to make all these decisions as a family. Open a saving and investment account together. And control it together. If the children are of age to understand, make them participate as well. Explain well the purpose of this account and educate them to learn to save. They will learn to understand that you can live comfortably with less. Encourage them to offer ideas about how to spend intelligently. They will thank you for the rest of their lives.

— GOAL 4 —

DO NOT HAVE DEBT AT THE TIME OF RETIREMENT

Not having debts when you retire means that you have paid all your debts including your mortgage and as much as possible the car loan, credit cards and any other loan that you have. Try to establish the discipline to keep only one credit card (CC) for your normal monthly expenses and pay the total balance each month. Credit cards should be used as a convenience to help manage your monthly expenses. When you have no debt, you have achieved half of your financial freedom.

Without debt a large part of your income will be free to finance your expenses during retirement. In addition, having no debt at retirement means the amount of capital or savings that you must accumulate in your pension funds, in addition to the social security pension, may be less than what you had originally calculated.

To reach this debt-free goal we need to manage our debts well while working. From age 25 to 65 we work hard to get salaries and other income. Large and unnecessary debt takes an important part of our income to pay interest, commissions, fines, fees and other payments for the credit cards and other loans. Surely you do not want to work all your life to enrich the banks and financial institutions and finish at retirement with nothing, in other words, in poverty.

The unfortunate thing is that part of one´s debt is frequently created from buying things that one does not need or that can be substituted for things of less price and quality. These purchases may satisfy cravings instead of taking care of real needs. Such purchases are a true financial crime that you make against yourself.

It is important to internalize deep in your mind the need to accumulate capital. That capital must generate enough income (interest, dividends, capital gains) for living in dignity when you don't work anymore. The only way to accumulate capital is by saving and investing intelligently. Remember the magic of compound interest. See the chapter "Investment Strategy" at the end of the book.

WHY DO WE GET INTO DEBT?

We are indebted because we have needs that must be addressed by resorting to loans from banks or financial institutions. Those institutions advance the necessary capital to acquire the goods or services that we need or want at that specific time such as:

- Credit card bills for regular expenses
- Loans to buy a car
- Student loans
- Mortgages
- Loans using your house as collateral (Home Equity Loans)
- Other personal loans
- Guarantees of loans for other people.

We must be aware that commerce has created a culture of consumerism in which we participate almost unconsciously. We get into debt because "everyone" gets into debt to buy what others buy. We do not want to have less. At least we want to have the same. The more expensive the item the more we attract attention and the better we look and feel.

But, it's so easy to get into debt. We think that the monthly payments for the CC will be so low. We imagine how good things the stores offer will look on us. The liquidation sales are spectacular because of their low prices. In addition, we are tempted with the variety of products that are offered with additional rebates if we will only request a new credit card in that store.

The demonstration effect and the social pressures in which we live from our earliest years have great influence on the way we buy and consume.

From our childhood we observe how our parents buy. They take us to supermarkets, malls and shopping centers. Sometimes it is considered a stroll, something for the family to do and be entertained.

But in the background the children observe, even when they seem distracted. They observe how the mother or father, or both behave in a department store, examining clothes, shoes, kitchenware, perfumes, tools, sporting goods and so many other things that are available. They listen to conversations between parents about what to buy, why, how much it costs, how to pay for it, etc.

In the children's minds parents are creating memories and experiences which constitute a deep education as a consumer. Over time it becomes a culture of purchase and a pattern of consumption that can be beneficial or harmful to them based on the examples of their parents.

Not only parents pass on their behavior to their children. Relatives, friends, classmates at the school and university, colleagues at work, and people who accompany them in their social life also influence their decisions about purchases and consumption. The young absorb these influences which may carry into adulthood. As adults they may want to have a personal identity like others in their social group: clothes, shoes, watches, smart phones, electronic tablets, haircuts, music, movies, television, etc.

The strategy of the business community is that commercial companies seek to make available to consumers the widest variety of products and services at the lowest possible prices as soon as possible so they offer credit plans having very low monthly payments for a long period of time. The idea is that everyone wins: consumers with low prices and with the possibility of immediately having the products they want, companies with high profits, banks with high interest, and the government with high income from sales taxes.

The above is true up to a certain point, but only when the consumer buys products or services they really need. It is not good when the purchase is just a whim or impulse buying because the buyer is persuaded by the extraordinary sales technology of commercial companies. In the end neither the so-called low prices nor the payment plans are always beneficial for the consumer.

The consumer always is bombarded by commercial propaganda in all media, be it TV at home, radio in cars, newspapers and magazines, business brochures distributed free of charge by mail. It is difficult for a person or a family to fight all the temptations that come their way.

Sales techniques are today very advanced, and are based on economic, psychological, cultural, ethnic, racial, age, and local studies and analysis. It is very difficult for an individual to overcome these influences.

In the 21st century it is now possible to analyze huge amounts of information through massive computers and increasingly sophisticated software. Every day the business community studies information about purchases from invoices, sales tickets, credit cards, bank accounts, etc. For them these are data sources (as if they were real gold mines) from which valuable information can be extracted to improve decisions about production, distribution, financing and sale of their products.

Financial institutions and banks that issue credit cards can examine purchases made by people at any moment.

Supermarkets examine in detail, product by product, what was sold in a day. They can do it by the hour, minute, second. For them this is very important because they must restock, calculate profits by product, examine what is sold or not sold, changes in the tastes of people, etc. As the supermarkets are in neighborhoods with well-defined characteristics, they can select products for that clientele, establish prices, focus commercial propaganda and other selling technologies.

This is true also of the big department stores that sell all kinds of products and the gigantic companies that supply them. The latter also directly flood society with commercial propaganda.

Commercial companies are improving their sales techniques and commercial propaganda aided by a technology that advances dramatically every year. Not only has the "shopping experience" improved in malls where they offer all kinds of services, presentations, entertainment, products in beautifully-lit store spaces and attractive and always changing sales designs. This also comes through the internet in online "shopping" website which are easy to access all over the world.

In recent years the development of sales or purchases "online" has advanced dramatically. Consumers, in addition to being exposed to the commercial campaigns of department stores or malls, are now exposed to countless virtual stores through the internet. On their website sellers (Amazon, Wal-Mart, Sears, JC Penney, etc.) offer a wide variety of products and services, accompanied by photos and commercial information, shipment options, prices of similar products, return forms, available credit, forms of payment and other features that make it easy to buy.

It is fair to conclude that for the consumer it is almost impossible to overcome the temptations offered by commercial and financial companies. But a consumer more educated and aware of their financial situation can control these temptations.

TYPES OF DEBT

There are debts that we might call necessary (some call them good debts), such as those you must assume to achieve long-term objectives, such as a mortgage to buy a house. Even so, these "good" debts must be in proportion to your income to be manageable.

As you pay your mortgage, you reduce your debt and at the same time the house is acquiring value. In addition, the house gives you a "free" service because you do not pay rent and you can also deduct the mortgage interest from your taxes if you itemize. The combined effect results in an accumulation of important capital for a family or individual. The chapter on mortgages below analyzes in detail this type of debt and the assumptions behind capital accumulation considering the crisis of 2007 – 09 caused by low quality mortgages.

We could also classify personal loans as "good" debts if you buy tools or other work-related things essential for your profession or trade. These could include photographic equipment, architecture implements, cooking utensils, garden maintenance machinery, etc. This equipment allows you to generate income to pay off the debt. Tax systems allow you to recover part of the financial expenses through incentives and depreciation.

"Good" debts are also those that you create using your credit card during the month to pay for basic family consumption (supermarket, pharmacy, etc.) and pay them completely at the end of the month. The total payment of the balance at the end of the month prevents you from having to pay interest. Less than a debt for you is a convenience that saves you from having to carry a lot of money in your wallet.

Debts to finance vocational, technical or university studies to achieve personal development and expand your ability to earn income are good debts too. The important thing is to know how to minimize these loans by going first to grants, scholarships, subsidies, donations, schoolwork programs and finally loans. The federal government, states, counties and cities offer programs in almost all these categories. The same may be available from corporations, non-profit organizations and possibly your family.

Unnecessary and costly debts (some call them "bad" debts) are those that you create to buy things or services to satisfy a craving rather than a need. If you continue buying things and services that are not true needs and paying only the minimum at the end of the month, this type of debt becomes eternal and accumulates quickly because of the interest and other expenses that the credit card company can charge you.

Other debts that I would consider low quality are those that occur when:

- Buying vehicles at a price that is not in proportion to your income. For example, instead of buying a car equivalent to a Toyota Corolla enough to meet your needs and that of your family you buy an SUV or flashy pick-up truck.

- Purchase other items such as electronic equipment (56 plasma TV), kitchen appliances, power tools, and other products that are very high priced and beyond of what your income allows. For you they are luxury goods. You could select items of lesser quality and price to avoid getting indebted beyond what is manageable. You fool yourself into thinking that by putting it on the credit card the minimum monthly payments will be very small and long-term without thinking that these payments are largely interest and commissions for which they have lent you the money.

- Short-term loans with local lenders who advance money against your salary with high interest rates, fines and commissions.

WHAT CAN WE DO TO CONTROL DEBT?

Let's not forget that today the other side of the spending medal is debt, especially from credit cards. If we want to control debt, we must control expenses. Therefore, *we must consume less and do so more intelligently. We must get used to living with less.* Here the key word is frugality.

Frugality does not mean living miserably. It is about consuming in an intelligent way: buying what is necessary in quality and quantity, avoiding waste and the useless and costly accumulation of things that we do not need.

We must learn to live at a level of consumption a little below what would correspond to our income. This is one of the most valuable secrets of those who are now millionaires.

What we consume reflects our level of maturity, personal lifestyle, common sense and good judgment. It is our projection to the world that surrounds us: home, car, clothes, food, ornaments, accessories.

BEFORE TAKING A LOAN READ THIS

In general, loans are contracts that you sign with banks or other financial organizations to receive a certain amount of money which you agree to pay in full by a certain period plus a percentage of interest back to the lender.

Loans can be very complex and varied. For example, there are automatically renewable, long-term loans such as mortgages and loans to buy cars, there are short and medium-term individual loans, etc. In this document we refer to the most common loans used by families and individuals: credit cards and car loans. The issue of mortgages, because of its importance in the formation of family or individual capital, is treat as a separate goal: Goal 5: "Have the house paid at the time of retirement."

Let's review now some elementary concepts that you need to understand well before signing a contract.

How important is your need to acquire a loan? It's crazy to get a loan to buy things or services that are beyond what is reasonable given your level of income. Or to buy products or services that you could do without. Or buying things that are more a craving than a need (bad debts).

What score do you have on your credit report? The credit report indicates what has been your financial behavior in the past and near present. It represents your financial trail and a facet of your character as a consumer. A good credit report usually has more than 650 points out of a total of 850. Low scores mean that you are a person with high financial risk (it is presumed that you are going to have trouble paying your debts) and therefore you must pay, as compensation, higher interest rates, have stronger loan conditions and higher fines. In other words, you have an important task ahead of improving your score if yours is low and make a great effort to avoid acquiring more loans because they will be very expensive.

Amount of the loan. My preference is to try to limit a loan to the lowest possible amount and to minimize the amount of interest you must pay. The golden rule is to minimize the amount of money you owe.

Interest rate. It is important to look for the lowest interest rate possible. In the long term, a small difference on an interest rate has a big consequence in what you will ultimately pay. Always remember that personal interest rates depend on your personal credit report.

Term of the loan. The longer the term, the more interest you will pay. This happens, for example, such as when buying a vehicle or when you keep high balances on credit cards and only pay the minimum at the end of the month. The problem is that we all have the tendency to deceive ourselves when we obsess over something. Lower minimum payments make us think that it will be easier to pay what we buy. But be aware of the cost: loan terms may make us pay huge amounts of money in interest and, in addition, depending on your financial history, on commissions and other charges.

Other loan conditions. Loans may have other conditions that you must know before you sign. For example, perhaps you can pay in advance part or all the loan without fines. What are the commissions, administrative expenses and fees that you must pay to process the loan? What are the fines that you must pay for late payments, etc.

We must remember that for banks and financial institutions the income from fines, commissions and other multiple charges they apply to consumers (credit cards, checking accounts) and savers (savings and investment accounts) are sometimes higher than the income they receive from the interest they charge on the loans. These institutions work to obtain the maximum amount of profit from their operations, including fines, interest and commissions. That is their legitimate mission. Your mission is to defend your income and invest what you can save.

You, as an individual, or part of a family, have very little time after your work and other responsibilities (children's activities, weekend errands, family entertainment, home repairs, etc.) to focus on reviewing periodically and in detail the account statements you receive from the several financial institutions that are part of your life, such as banks, credit cards, mortgages, utilities, and others. It becomes difficult to fully appreciate the costs of your loans. In addition, charges to your accounts are already added when you get the bill or monthly statement and many times we let them pass even if more analysis or action is required on our part, especially when the amount involved is small.

For many, the challenge is about defending our income from ourselves, from our impulses to spend everything we have without thinking about the future.

WHAT IS THE CREDIT REPORT?

The credit reports (CR) are an x-ray of your present financial situation and an analysis of your financial behavior. It is a valuable instrument for financial institutions when making decisions about your credit application.

Credit reports are produced by private companies and used by all institutions that provide loans. They measure financial risk, essential information for financial institutions. With these reports financial institutions are able to evaluate if you are going to pay your loan or credit card in full and on time based on your prior history of paying.

Take care to understand very well the meaning of your credit report as it will affect your economic life for a long period of time, for better or for worse. Financial and other decisions depend on the credit report, be it to buy a car, a mortgage, a credit card, obtain a job, become a member of a club, rent a house, etc.

The credit report says many things about you, the most important being your willingness and ability to pay your debts on time. It also says something important about your character and social behavior. The institutions with which you interact want to know how indebted you are, how many credit cards you have, how many car loans, how big your mortgage is, how long you will be in debt, what is the relationship of your debts to your income, if they are consumer debts or a mortgage or car loan.

They also want to know certain conditions of their loans: if they are loans only in your name or if you have been endorsing other people's loans; terms payments, balance owed, monthly amount you must pay, interest rate you are paying, who are your creditors, etc.

This information is used by institutions jointly with other information obtained from other sources such as income from employment (certified by your employer), your income tax return, from when you were employed by your current employer, other work you have had. Depending on what you are applying for (for example, a job) it is very possible that they also will request other information e.g., about whether you have had problems with civil or criminal justice, or if you travel, where and for what period, etc.

Other information sources that are used by many institutions include online information about you such as in Facebook, LinkedIn, Google, Twitter, YouTube, Blogs, your own website, etc.

All this information can be acquired by the institution or person with whom you are establishing a financial or work relationship. The kind of information may vary in quantity or quality depending on the information needs of those institutions or people.

Institutions that commonly use this type of information include the following: banks and financial institutions, department and retail stores, service companies (TV/cable, telephone, electricity, water.), companies or people who rent property, insurance companies, private sector employers, government institutions.

The Credit Report is prepared by commercial companies which obtain or buy information about customers from several different financial institutions in the country. The three best-known companies or credit bureaus are: EQUIFAX, TRANSUNION and EXPERIAN. They process this information and sell it to their customers. These customers can be institutions of all kinds as discuss above that require information about you to close a transaction.

These companies have been expanding their services and selling them more and more to their institutional and individual clients and yourself. That is, you can buy credit report information about yourself for a price. If you pay more, you receive more information services and protection of your identity.

It is important that you review your credit report on a regular basis to verify that no errors have been made in your data. More important, is the need to verify that nobody has opened credit cards or requested a loan in your name in a fraudulent manner. In other words, they have not stolen your identity to apply for loans or other financial services.

Normally when a company requests a credit report about you, they are obtaining a credit report from the three main credit bureaus noted above. The reports are relatively similar because most use the same sources of information. However, it is possible that there are some differences due to delays in processing information, errors made in its registration or some differences in the way each one calculates scores.

The most important value of the credit report is the score that is periodically assigned to your individual account. The score is presented in the form of a number that summarize all that can be said about you and your finances.

The scoring system is called FICO (Fair Isaac Corporation). This system is used almost universally by banks and other financial institutions. Each time you apply for a loan, you will most likely be asked for your FICO score. These scores fluctuate between 300 and 850 points. The higher your score the more value your financial background has. Having a score above 650 has several advantages:

- You can get a loan with better financing conditions: lower interest rate, better terms, lower commissions, fees and other administrative expenses.

- In addition, you can get your loan more quickly which is important if you are getting a mortgage or buying a vehicle. For example: if you buy a $20,000 vehicle with a FICO of 750, you may be charged 5% interest and pay $377 monthly or a total of $2,645 in interest. If you have a FICO of 589 you are likely to be charged interest of 15.4% and pay monthly about $480 for a total of $8,778 in interest on the $20,000.

- If your score is low, you become a person of "high financial risk" which means that it will be more difficult for you to obtain a loan and if you get it you will have to pay high interest rates.

- In addition, with a low score you will have to pay higher premiums for car insurance, mortgage and other insurance that you need.

- Banks use your credit report to determine if they are going to grant you a mortgage, what interest rate they will apply and other loan terms.

- You could be limiting your employment opportunities if you have a low score. As we saw earlier, more and more human resources offices use records collected from various sources, an important one being the credit bureaus. However, in the case of employment your credit score probably will not be decisive in their decision.

FACTORS THAT INFLUENCE THE CALCULATION OF YOUR SCORE.

- Number of loans you have open: credit cards, car loans, mortgages, commercial loans, approved bank overdrafts.

- Amount in dollars of all your loans.
- Information about arrears in the payment of your loans.
- Data about bank accounts kept open and checks that have been returned due to lack of funds, arrears in payments, fines.
- The same in relation to credit cards: monthly payments that are overdue, fines you have received, number of times you have paid in arrears.
- The same in relation to all public utility services: electricity, water, sewerage, telephone, cable, and other routine utility bills.
- The late payment or nonpayment of rent of the property where you live.
- The late payment or nonpayment of common services where you live such as condo fees.

Keep in mind that negative information is kept in your registry for 7 years. Bankruptcy statements are kept for 10 years. Information about overdue but paid accounts is maintained for 7 years from the date of the last payment. Fortunately, positive information remains indefinitely.

Factors that do not affect your credit report.

- Demographic factors such as religion, age, gender, ethnicity, marital status, salary, type of occupation, work history.
- The type of interest rate you are currently paying or if you are using a consulting firm that is helping you overcome your debt problems.

- The consultations that the corporations have about your credit score, only for background or to grant credit.

How to improve your score.

- The most direct and immediate way is to pay back all delinquent debts and continue paying all your debts on time.

- In the case of credit cards, it is important to maintain a balance at the end of the month of no more than 50% of the limit that you have approved.

- Another way is to keep your oldest accounts active, even with a small balance to build up a long record of paying on time.

- Limit the number of accounts you have open and avoid continuing to submit credit applications.

- Avoid signing an endorsement of debts for relatives and friends.

Avoid errors in your credit reports.

- From time to time, credit companies make mistakes which can sometimes be very difficult to correct.

- Those mistakes can be because you changed your name (e.g. through marriage or adoption) or because you have a very common name (John Smith).

- It can also complicate your report if you change your address often or your spouse's bills are handled together with yours.

- Finally, there may be human errors when you write up information in your account.

Types of errors

- Information about your identity may be incorrect. These errors can be in terms of your name, place of birth, social security number, driver's license or other basic identifying information.

- Your work history may include corporations in which you never worked. It may also be that the company where you worked has errors in your personnel records.

- Sometimes corporations require information about a person who has never applied for a loan or service.

- In your credit report there are accounts that you never opened, or that you already paid and closed, or that are duplicated or have disappeared.

- The shortest way to solve these problems is to call the claims offices of the credit companies: EQUIFAX (1-866-238-8067), TRANSUNION (1-800-916-8800), EXPERIAN (https://www.experian.com/)

CREDIT CARDS

Nowadays it is extremely important that you learn how credit cards work so that you can use most effectively the advantages they offer while avoiding their disadvantages.

Remember one main thing: the bigger the monthly balances that you carry over the bigger the interest you pay and the harder it is for you to pay off this debt. If you fall behind in payment or do not pay the minimum amount that corresponds each month, you are vulnerable to fines, commissions, higher interest rates, lower rating in your credit report. The latter can affect you in many ways. See previous paragraphs.

Remember also that your debt is growing in a way similar to a compound interest rate. This means that, if you pay the minimum, the interest rate will be applied to the balance owed (which includes accrued interest that is carried along with your debt) plus the purchases made that payment period, normally monthly.

WHAT IS A CREDIT CARD?

In general terms, the classic credit card (CC) is a contract that you sign with a financial or commercial corporation to obtain a loan to buy products or services and pay the loan back in installments. Some of the best-known financial corporations are Citibank, Bank of America, Wells Fargo, and SunTrust. Other financial corporations are VISA, MASTERCARD, CAPITAL ONE, DISCOVERY, AMERICAN EXPRESS.

To obtain a credit card you must fill out an application form where they ask for information about you: your name, address, telephone number, e-mail address, if you rent or own your home, social security number, ID or driver's license number, company where you work (your employer), other income you receive, and other information depending on the financial corporation offering the credit card. Once the application is approved, the credit card is mailed to your address. You must activate it by calling the phone number that comes taped to the card. Then you must sign it in the back before using it.

The financial or commercial corporation opens an account in which they accumulate the details of each purchase you made during the month, the balance due that month, interest you must pay, commissions and fines that have been charged and any other information that the institution wants to communicate back to you.

The process of obtaining a credit card has been simplified since 2013. As of that year economic conditions were improving, and corporations began to issue more credit cards with fewer requirements. You should avoid losing your credit card. Nor should you give your credit card number to strangers or have it copied without your authorization. There is a lot of fraud using cards stolen or copied by thieves or people trying to use someone else's card illegally.

Credit cards have a magnetic tape on the back where important information about you has been filed. From 2016, credit cards also have an electronic chip where your information is more secure. As mentioned above, once the card is signed you can start using it. At the end of the month you must pay what you owe in full, in part, or only the minimal required payment as stated in the bill. When you pay only part the card works like a loan which is renewed every month.

It is important to remember that when you activate a credit card you receive the right to buy or carry out other financial transactions up to a certain limit of money. For example, you may have a CC with a limit of $1,000. If at the end of the month the balance you owe is $200 you have $800 left to spend. If you pay $200 your limit goes back to $1,000.

Corporations manage their credit cards in groups of days equivalent to one month. Your payment date may be different from a calendar month. In other words, the billing period may not close on the 30th or 31st of each month, but on any other day, according to the date which the company decides your payment is due, normally the date the credit card was approved, or your account was opened.

For example: your billing period may go from March 18 to April 18. In the monthly billing statement, you receive by regular mail or electronic mail, you are told what balance you owe and when you must pay it. Approximately 20 days are given to pay the balance either in full or at least the minimum. That minimum can usually be between 1% and 2% of the balance you owe that month.

New regulations require that the status of a credit card account must indicate how much you should pay in interest if you only pay the minimum and how long it will take to pay the entire balance. I found an example of this in an article in Kiplinger's magazine on personal finance (excellent magazine, by the way).

In that example, it is indicated that if a person has a balance of $2,000 with an interest rate of 22% and pays only $40 monthly it will take more than 11 years to pay off that debt plus interest of $3,471. In total, the $2,000 balance plus the $3,271 interest comes to $5,271. It is not good to continue to be indebted.

Following this example, if you continue using that card with the same interest rate and monthly payment, you will remain indebted perhaps for the rest of your life. I do not think you want to work all your life to enrich financial corporations.

ADVANTAGES AND DISADVANTAGES OF THE CREDIT CARD

A credit card offers many advantages, some of the most important being the following:

- It is not necessary to carry money with you avoiding several types of risks.

- It is easy to use for all kinds of payments in stores or purchases through the internet, to withdraw money in banks or some stores, for emergencies, etc. It is a great convenience.

- In case you lose it, or it is stolen, it is easy to cancel and get a new one. At the same time, it is easy to cancel a payment when it has been fraudulent, or a product has been damaged or is the wrong item.

- At the end of the month you receive an account statement with the details of your payments. This information allows you to review everything you bought in the month, financial charges (interest, commissions, fines), the total balance of what you owe and the minimum you must pay. The purpose of this information is for you to verify the payments charged and pay what you owe.

Credit cards also have some disadvantages:

- Perhaps the biggest disadvantage is how easy it is for a person to obtain one or several credit cards. This has led many people to easily borrow or increase their debts without having a clear idea of the financial burden they are creating.

- It is becoming easier to be a victim of identity theft from a credit card. If it is stolen or you lose it, you are vulnerable to being charged for purchases you have not made. Sometimes they steal only the information without you realizing it, for example, when you pay in a restaurant an employee may easily copy your information. This type of fraud can be easy to detect at the end of the month if you carefully review the credit card statement, which you should get in the habit of doing every month.

- Sometimes these purchases go unnoticed because they charge small sums that you do not detect when you review your account statement. Another fraudulent case occurs when you buy a service for a limited period, for example, a month or a year (say for a magazine), and the company continues to charge you the same amount every month. When you call them, they may say it was just a mistake or that they have an auto renew tied to the service and they will return the money. But if you do not review your account statement well every month these charges may go unnoticed for a long period of time or forever.

- In other cases, it can be very difficult for you to recover those fraudulent payments because the company disappeared or is based abroad. Therefore, evaluate well the pros and cons if you decide to set up automatic payments on your credit card or through your checking account.

- If you do not pay the amount required when due your credit report will be affected (your score will go down). This means that the interest rates you are paying or those for new loans will be higher and their conditions will be less favorable to you.

HOW MUCH DOES IT COST TO HAVE A CREDIT CARD?

Credit cards are one of the best financial businesses of banks and financial institutions. Income from commissions and fines is one of their main sources of profit. When you have a credit card you must pay interest for what you owe, commissions for financial services that you received in that month and fines if you do not comply with the terms of the contract.

INTEREST RATES. Credit cards charge different interest rates depending on the type of transaction you make. These rates depend on several factors and one of the most important is the score in your Credit Report. As we saw earlier that score (FICO) can fluctuate between 350 and 850 points. The lower your score the higher the interest you will pay for a loan.

For example, in the month of June 2018, a major bank offered credit cards with the following annual interest rates depending on one's FICO score. The best interest went to the best scores:

- For purchases: 13.99%; 15.99%; 17.99%; 19.99; 21.99%

- For transfers: 13.99%; 15.99%; 17.99%; 19.99%; 21.99%

- For money advances: 25.24%

According to the above, the interest rate applied to a person with a good credit score, say above 750 points, will be the lowest rate: 13.99%. Now, look closely—the difference in interest between a good and bad score is 8% (21.99% minus 13.99%). That difference represents thousands of dollars more for a low credit score that you will have to pay in the long term for debt you keep on your credit card.

Let's see now how the interest rate is applied by the credit card company. They do it by dividing the annual interest rate by 365 days to determine the daily interest that will be applied to your daily balance. If we divide 13.99% (assuming you have the best or lowest interest rate) for 365 days, that daily interest will be 0.038329%.

For example, at the beginning of the day (say July 10), the company will take the balance of your account from the previous day (July 9) and will add all the purchases and other transactions that you made on this day (July 10). To this total they will add the interest of this day (0.038329%) to determine your new balance at the end of this day (July 10). They charge you interest because the credit card company CC is lending you the money to pay for your purchases or perform other transactions such as money transfers, check cashing or cash withdrawal.

What they cannot add to that total are the commissions and fines they have charged that day because those charges are not a loan and therefore the regulations forbid it.

Let's see an example of transactions made on July 10:

Balance as of July 9:	$100.00
Purchases made on July 10,	$60.00
Transfer you make to a bank account.	$40.00
Advance of money you got when you bought something:	$25.00
Subtotal	$225.00
Interest of the day (0.038329) on $200:	0.77
Interest of the day (0.069151%) on $25:	0.17
Balance at the end of the day	$225.94

The advance of money for $25 has an annual rate of 25.24% for which the daily rate is 0.069151% (25.24 divided by 365).

Look carefully at the new balance. This contains the interest payments of the 10th of July. That balance will be used the next day to make the same calculations. This means that you will have to pay interest on all the transactions you make on July 11 plus the balance of July 10, which already contains interest for that day. In other words, at the end of July 11, you will be paying interest on the interest that was charged the previous day: July 10.

The credit card may have a fixed interest for a certain period, for example, when promotions or special offers are made for the purchase of something. Or a lower fixed special interest rate may be offered (in some cases the card is offered without payment of interest) for one year if a new credit card is opened. These rates are usually better than ordinary rates.

But you must be very careful because if you do not pay on time under that special offer, they can start charging you the ordinary rate. This requires that you read very carefully all the details and fine print contained in the contracts you sign with the credit card company and very carefully review the account statements sent to you at the end of the month with all the transactions, interest, fines and commissions.

The interest rate can also be variable, that is, consisting of two parts which can vary at any time. The first part is a special rate called "Prime Rate" which is offered to corporations that are the best rated for paying their debts. This is a rate that is calculated every day and published in the financial sections of the main newspapers including the Wall Street Journal, a newspaper specializing in economic and financial matters. Currently that rate is around 3.5%.

With the prime rate, the credit card companies add an additional or marginal rate, which depends on market conditions and your score on the credit report. These rates are already show above for purchases, transfers and money advances. For example, the 13.99% rate for purchases offered to the best debtors consists of 3.5% (prime rate) plus 10.49% (additional or marginal rate).

IMPORTANT: **These rates can be changed by the bank that issued the credit card if there are changes in regulations, in your Credit Report, or in financial market conditions, or for any other reason.**

IMPORTANT: **One of the latest published regulations states that changes in interest rates apply only to new debts. The balances that you owed with the previous rates continue with those rates.**

IMPORTANT: **if you pay the total amount owed at the end of the month, you pay no interest. You can use the credit card and benefit from all its advantages (such as not having to carry money and be protected in case of fraud) and at the end of the month pay no interest.**

FINES: If you do not pay at least the minimum monthly balance of your debt, the credit card company will charge you a fine that can vary between $15 and $35 depending on the size of the debt balance and the contract you have with the financial institution that granted the card. The value of the fine is added to the balance of what you already own. If you continue not paying on time in the following months the fine could be $38.

It is important to note that if you pay, but pay late, that does not free you from the fine. The fine is also a bad item in your financial history. In most cases a late payment is not reported to the credit institutions, but if that situation repeats itself it is reported.

Another situation is one in which you pay, but the check (or other form of payment) is returned for lack of funds. In this case you must pay $27 and if you continue with this problem you must pay $38 each time the payment is returned. Even if you ask for the check to be sent back to you and you then pay it, you still will have this fine. The value of the fine is added to the balance of what you owe.

Because of these problems the credit card company may increase the interest rate on your debt as a punishment. This rate can be up to 29.99% per year, the highest interest rate that the credit card company can charge you under the current regulations. This interest rate could continue to be charged to your account indefinitely. This is the worst fine because in the long term it means a huge additional cost to you for using the card.

WHAT HAPPENS IF I DO NOT PAY?

One thing is to pay late, something else is simply not to pay. In the latter case, not only is the situation reported to the credit bureaus but also to collection agencies. The latter can force you to return the merchandise, especially if it is a car, TV and other product of great value. And, of course, the debt begins to accumulate interest and fines in your account, substantially increasing each month the balance of what you owe until the day you pay, return the merchandise and settle a debt.

COMMISSIONS. Commissions are payments that are charged when you make a withdrawal, transfer money, or make another financial transaction that involves an advance of money. The following are examples:

- Take money out of an ATM: you pay 5% of the value of the transaction or a minimum of $10. When you use a debit card, you do not pay commission.

- Transfer of funds: if you request a transfer to pay a debt with another institution, there is a charge of 4% for each transfer or a minimum of $10.

- Direct deposit: if you transfer money from your credit card to a deposit account (checking account, savings account, pension fund, etc.) you will be charged 4% for each transfer or a minimum of $10.

- Transfer of money electronically to a deposit account. In this case you will be charged 5% or a minimum of $10.

- Credit card check: if you sign a check against your credit card you must pay 4% of the value of each check or a minimum of $10.

- Advance money: the credit card will charge you 5% for each transaction with a minimum of $10. Transactions include to get money from a bank, or a prepaid check, make an electronic money transfer, buy traveler's checks. You can also get money from a non-financial institution such as a supermarket or department store.

- Protection against overdrafts: If you use your credit card to transfer funds to your checking account when you do not have enough funds to cover a check (in other words, to avoid an overdraft) the credit card company will charge you 5% or a minimum of $10.

- Purchase foreign currency: When you are abroad and use your credit card to obtain local currency or when you are in the US and buy something abroad you must pay a commission of 2% of the dollar value of this transaction plus other commissions or interest that may apply.

OTHER TYPES OF CREDIT CARDS

Commercial or customer cards are those offered by commercial companies such as Target, Wal-Mart, Sears, JC Penney, etc. These are the cards that the cashier offers you when you are going to pay. The normal thing is that they offer a 10 to 25% additional discount for that purchase if you obtain a credit card at that time.

These offers are a great temptation for the discounts and benefits they promise and one of the ways in which clients end up having several credit cards. In the long run several credit cards can end up with debts beyond what is prudent.

Debit or bank cards (Debit Cards) are issued by the bank in which you have your checking account. When you use this card the value of your purchase is immediately charged to your bank checking account, electronically. It is as if you had made a check to pay for your purchase. Since you are using your own money (the money you have is your checking account) you do not pay interest.

You must be clear that the limit on your use of this card is equal to the balance you have in that checking account. If you overdraw you must pay a commission or fine. Keep in mind that for various reasons some companies such as hotels and car rental companies. do not accept debit cards. You should consider that this card has less protection against fraud than a regular credit card.

An important aspect to keep in mind is that the charges you make by check and debit card come mixed in your checking account monthly statement. In some cases, they are separated into these two groups. To keep good track of your current account balance at the end of the month you must record the checks you write in your checkbook register (where you write down the details of the check each time you write one) and you should do the same for debit card charges with the copies of the invoices given by the companies where you made purchases.

It is also a good idea to write in your checkbook register a short note about the purchase you made using the debit card. At the end of the month you then can check your checking account balance with your checkbook register because it contains not only the checks you wrote but also all your purchases with the debit card. In addition, you can check that the card purchases match the invoices.

A problem could arise when you do not keep track of debit card purchases. You can practically lose control of this account and overdraw. This is bad for you, but very good for financial corporations because they can charge you up to $35 for each check or card purchase that produces an overdraft. This can also mean that the interest rate charged may increase and, in addition, it will be necessary to pay other administrative expenses and fines for late payments.

An important effect of these overdrafts, if you do them repeatedly, is that companies making the credit reports will be informed. They may lower your credit score, which can hurt you any time you apply for a loan.

In addition, if you do not keep track of your check or debt card charges you make against your checking account you have no way to identify any charges that shouldn't be there either because of bank error or fraud. It is very possible that they go unnoticed and you will pay them.

One approach to this issue is to use the debit card only to withdraw money from the ATM so that it is easier to check your checking account balance at the end of the month. For all other expenses you can use one classic credit card, only one. The worst thing you can do is have too many credit cards. Not only can you get into huge debt it also become almost impossible to control, leaving you vulnerable to all the negative effects mentioned above.

WHAT CAN BE DONE TO BETTER MANAGE CREDIT CARDS?

My advice is to try to get rid of most credit cards. Keep only one for regular household expenses and pay it in full at the end of the month.

One way to start closing credit cards is by looking for additional ways to generate income to pay off balances. For example, get a second job, drastically reduce expenses, start paying for purchases with cash or debit cards, have garage sales which not only give you a little income but force you to think about non-essential purchases you made in the past while freeing up space in your home.

With some extra income or by saving more the card balances can be paid and the accounts closed, improving your credit rating, avoiding more interest payments and learning to be more economical. There are many people who simply cut up the cards to stop using them. But remember that you must continue paying until you leave the balance at zero before requesting its closure. Remember also that it is very easy to open an account, but very difficult to close one. Those who offer the credit card do everything possible so that you do not close it.

You can initiate the process of closing a credit card account on the internet. But it is common to be asked to make a telephone call. We already know that calling by phone is not easy. It requires a lot patience and time. But do it, it's the best gift you can give yourself. And above all do not request another credit card even if they offer new terms. Simply put a large NO in your mind to avoid temptation.

From the very beginning the credit card has promoted a lifestyle of high consumption that was greatly facilitated by paying very low monthly installments (usually a little more than 1% of the monthly balance owed). At the same time this system results in paying high interest rates even more than 30% per year over the outstanding balance.

Many people acquire several credit cards and use all the credit granted, generating a standard of living much higher than can be maintained by their real income. Be honest with yourself when determining "needs". It is very possible that some things we consider essential today, after some analysis, we discover we can live without or replace with similar one's of lesser cost.

As mentioned above, I encourage the idea of having a garage sale to make some extra pocket money and to get a sense a what you really need. And how you can focus on what is essential and what is over-consumption. It is a matter of looking in the garage and seeing mechanical, carpentry, electrical, and garden tools that are still waiting to be used. The same with kitchen items and other things that we accumulate over time and rarely use. They are there just in case we need them. The same goes for clothing, shoes, bathrooms items, and other home accessories that we have collected over the years. It is a matter of looking in our closets and kitchen cupboards to find things we no longer use or never used.

So many purchases fall into the impulsive shopping category. They are bought when we are distracted, tired or depressed and suddenly we see items that seem cheap, "useful" and make us feel good at the moment.

When it's time to move is when you arrive at the moment of truth. How to get rid of so much junk? If we apply the criteria of how many times per year we use what we buy we could probably get rid of a lot of things.

In summary, do not spend more than you earn. Have the company where you work automatically deposit into your savings and investment account at least 10% of the check you receive at the end of the month to cover emergencies. That leaves you with less salary for expenses. But this does not mean you can spend that remaining amount foolishly or impulsively.

SOME ADDITIONAL TIPS

Make a list of the things you buy every day. This will keep you aware of how you are spending your money. Maintain and review all sales receipts. Check them regularly so that you have a good sense about how the money was expended. Remember that spending impulsively is an addiction that must be combated mentally, with that big NO in your mind.

Make a list of the expenses that are most important to you. Reduce other expenses, replace expensive items with others of lower cost, or postpone your purchase for later. Delaying a purchase is easier mentally than deciding not to buy at the moment, and this will give you time to think more deliberately about whether it's worth buying.

Always keep in mind that each time you use the credit card you are paying more than the price of your purchase unless you pay the entire bill each month. Interest, commissions, and fines can greatly increase the cost of what you buy, especially if you pay only a minimum every month.

Try using checks or your debit card instead of a credit card for necessary purchases. This will force you to limit your expenses to the balance you have in the bank. And you will appreciate more concretely how you spend your money especially if you pay in cash.

Try to pay off and eliminate first your credit card debts with high interest rates. Be more aggressive in paying them. Or start by paying off the credit card that has the lowest balance. And then close it. That will give you psychological support because it shows that you are effectively changing your spending behavior and taking control of your debts.

Look for a second job with the exclusive goal of paying off the debts you have on your credit cards and then close them. This is a good option because it allows you to appreciate the cost of spending money on unnecessary things.

Finally avoid using a line of credit against capital you have in your home. It is dangerous because after paying off the credit cards you may feel rich again and start getting into debt once more. In that situation you double your losses and leave yourself economically vulnerable at the time of your retirement.

Ultimately, it's about freeing yourself from being a prisoner of plastic money and gradually acquiring your financial freedom.

— GOAL 5 —

HAVE THE HOUSE PAID AND WITHOUT LIABILITIES

It is a good idea to have the house paid at the time of retirement or earlier if possible.

The goal is to arrive at retirement, whatever your age, without having the financial and psychological pressures of paying a mortgage or any other obligation that used your home as collateral. Achieving this goal means the income that was used to pay the mortgage now can be used for other purposes and have the house value totally in your ownership.

In the United States approximately 32% of the homeowners have fully paid their home at the time of retirement. Many of these homeowners are over 65 years of age. The official census shows that such owners begin to pay off their mortgages between the 45 and 54 years of age.

According to a survey conducted by the Harris Interactive Company (2016) about 40% of interviewed homeowners aged 55 or older said that the smartest decision they had made was to pay off their mortgage.

For many low and middle-income couples (despite having two incomes) this goal is not easy to achieve. They are aware that they must first pay off consumer debts (e.g. credit cards) that have high interest rates (up to about 30% per year) plus fines and commissions. In addition, they must raise capital in their pension and emergency funds to supplement the income they will receive from social security in order to retire with some economic security.

Keep in mind that as time passes, a working person or couple begins to receive more income from their jobs or business (wage increases, promotions, bonuses, more responsibility). This makes the amount of the mortgage, which is fixed normally for 30 years, represent a lower percentage of their total income. That situation also allows the individual or couple to cover other financial responsibilities mentioned on previous pages.

Statistics show that working couples are most likely to fully pay off their mortgage when they are in their 50s or 60s. This is when their income is higher, family expenses have been reduced as children reach some economic independence, other family debts have been pay off, and family expenses have finally reached a level that allows them to save a larger part of their income.

It is important to keep in mind, however, that interest on the mortgage can be deducted from one's income taxes which can be an important incentive to maintain the mortgage. But very few low and middle-income couples itemize their taxes because the standard deduction is usually higher.

Finally, having one's home paid off is a great psychological relief for working couples. It means that the property title is fully in their names and that the total value of the property is theirs. This is a moment of celebration because in addition to giving them significant economic security it also gives a sense of satisfaction, having achieved after much effort full ownership of their home and a place on Earth which they can call theirs.

Considering all the above, a working couple must analyze the pros and cons of having the house paid given their economic and psychological circumstances. Remember that they should also have the other goals to meet by the time they are ready for retirement.

WAYS TO PAY OFF A MORTGAGE

Some individuals and couples pay something extra every month to lower the mortgage principal more quickly. The monthly mortgage payment remains the same, but the number of years is reduced, and the amount of interest paid is reduced too.

In some cases, depending on the mortgage contract from time to time they may be able to pay an extra sum directly to the principal reducing the monthly mortgage payment, but the term of 30 years is maintained.

There are several combinations of alternatives that may be used by homeowners to pay off their mortgages early. The most common is a gradual process of paying extra of one's savings every month to be applied to the principal of the mortgage.

Here are some additional tips:

- Pay something extra on a regular basis, even a small amount, to lower the principal. For example, $50 monthly accumulates $600 annually or $6,000 in 10 years. On a mortgage of $120,000 this represents a significant extra payment.

- Allocate all wage increases, bonuses, overtime payments and other extra income to pay the principal of the mortgage. This is an effective option, but it requires maintaining one's consumption at the same level and avoiding borrowing such as through credit cards.

- Getting a second job. If this is done for 5 years, at the minimum wage of $7.25 an hour, for 10 hours a week you could accumulate $17,400 to pay extra on the mortgage and reduce at the same time your interest payment on the mortgage substantially. On a mortgage of $120,000 this represents a significant saving.

- If for some reason you receive a large sum of money (an inheritance, the sale of a fixed asset) or if you decide to sell one of your cars, you can apply that to reduce your monthly mortgage payment, again reducing substantially the interest payment during the period of the mortgage.

- If the mortgage rate in the market falls by 1% or more, you may be able to refinance your 30-year loan. Refinancing may generate significant savings in interest payments and if done for 15 years, such saving become substantial.

COST OF MAINTAINING A PAID HOUSE.

It is important to consider that once the mortgage is paid, the expenses of owning a house continue, but they are lower. In the case of a $120,000 mortgage, let's say the monthly payment was $573. This amount can now be used to increase your pension or emergency fund and pay other debts.

- Real estate taxes must continue to be paid. They grow annually.

- As will insurance against fires, floods or other events that homeowner's insurance normally covers. They grow with inflation and the age of the house.

- Repairs and ordinary maintenance of the house must continue. These expenses will continue to grow with inflation as needs change and the house ages.

- The same is normally true for the cost of public utility services such as electricity, water and sewage, TV, internet, phone landlines and other communication devices. Inflation affects all of them.

If income during retirement is able to be maintained at the same level as when you were working, plus annual adjustment for inflation and a minimum return on investment, there will be no problem maintaining a lifestyle like before retirement. But for most couples, once retired, the income decreases and owning a house can become a mayor economic burden.

Moving to a smaller and cheaper house or condo may be one solution. This reduces the expenses of maintaining a big house and paying large utility bills. This option also simplifies living when one's enters senior years.

Nevertheless, having your house paid gives you have greater flexibility to decide what to do when you retire. Do you want to retire in the place where you currently live or do you want to live elsewhere? Do you want to move to a smaller house or maintain a house with enough space for your children and grandchildren when they visit?

Some couples use the resources released from paying off the mortgage to help their family. Perhaps they want to help the children with the purchase of a house, the grandchildren pay for university, or provide economic support in case some calamity happens such as the loss of employment or health problems.

Finally, there is the alternative of selling the house, investing the value of the sale and renting a house or apartment. Leasing also has many advantages: no maintenance costs, no building insurance, no property taxes and perhaps some utility services that are the responsibility of the landlord.

— GOAL 6 —

RETIRE IN GOOD HEALTH AND ENERGY

Surely this is the most important goal. It is meaningless to be financially secure if we do not have good health to enjoy our life during retirement.

The new generations are more aware of the importance of creating good habits: what to eat, exercising on a regular basis, avoiding drugs, tobacco, alcohol, and other excesses. Fortunately, today there is better information and more educational opportunities about how to become and stay physically and mentally fit.

For those who are approaching 50, it is very likely that their doctors will begin to warn them about the need to control certain health conditions before they turn into chronic diseases, such as diabetes and heart disease. These are preventive warnings. They tell us it is time to think more seriously about what health means at retirement.

Health insurance continues to rise. The costs of health services are growing well above the general inflation rates and will continue to do so in the future. Not all health expenses are covered by insurance. There is always an exception, exclusion, co-payment, deduction or other payment condition that may directly or indirectly apply. The same applies to pharmaceutical expenses and other expenses that may not be fully covered by one's health insurance such as dental, eye and other specialized services.

Elderly care insurance for home care services, moving to senior homes, or long-term rehabilitation are not fully covered by MEDICARE. So, they must be purchased separately. These are expensive insurances and premiums increased considerably the later in life they are purchased especially if there are chronic diseases.

In light of the above, a mayor tip that I can share is to make a health plan with your doctor starting at age 50.

There is a lot written about this matter. Be well informed about your health risks, not only through your doctor but also by reading health publications that are readily available, many free of charge. Practicing good health habits every day is equivalent to making a deposit in your life account.

FINANCING CHILDREN'S HIGHER EDUCATION

As we recall in each chapter, the family economic goals at the time of retirement are: have enough resources in pension funds to retire in dignity, have an emergency fund, have social security and Medicare complete, have the house paid, live without debt and have good health at the time of retirement.

We cannot fail to recognize that higher education for the children is one of the most important goals and expenses of low- and middle-income families during their working lives. Most parents expect their children to go to a 4-year university or a 2-year community college to get a professional or technical license or trade that allows them to support themselves as adults. We all recognize that the best inheritance that can be left to children is good education and training. This is the assumption behind this chapter.

For many, higher education takes two or four years, but it may take longer depending on the academic skills of the student and their economic situation. In addition, some students will probably continue with postgraduate courses (masters, doctorates) or specialties that extend their years of studies and therefore their economic dependence on the family and other institutions that offer financing.

What is certain is that parents will be faced with the issue of financing at least part of their children's higher educational expenses. This situation is multiplied by the number of children.

There are several reasons that children's higher education expenses are not given the importance they deserve from the moment they are born or before, when the family is forming. An important reason is that the income of the parents may be very low as they begin their working life. In addition, they may have start-up expenses during the first decade of their joint life—they may be buying a house, paying two car loans if both work, creating an emergency fund, making contributions to their pension funds, paying loans from credit cards (for furniture, home accessories, new baby expenses, etc.). Maybe also they are still paying for the costs of their post-high school university or technical studies.

COSTS OF HIGHER EDUCATION

It is essential that you be well informed about how much it will cost to send your children to college. Any initial task is for you to find out how much it will cost for four years in a public university of the State where you reside. This information will be in today's dollars, which is a good basis for future calculations. It is important also to find out about the costs of higher education alternatives such as community or technical colleges, out-of-state universities, and some private universities. These data will help you to make comparisons of costs when planning the future education of your children.

It is very important that your children participate in obtaining this information once they are old enough, analyze and begin to set a realistic university goal given the economic situation of your family and the financial help that may be available within government and the private sector.

In addition, it must be recognized that university education expenses have been growing annually at a much higher rate than overall inflation. The average inflation over the last 20 years has been about 2% per year and that of education over the last 10 years has been from 8 to 10% per year. This contrast helps one see that it is absolutely necessary to start saving for your children's higher education as soon as possible in order to avoid or minimize the future economic stresses on family finances and help your children take advantage of possible opportunities.

Tuition fees, courses, health and life insurance, books, school supplies, transportation (perhaps including a car, auto insurance and associated expenses), food and lodging, clothing, entertainment, travel, computers, cellular phones and other expenses associated with the digital and cybernetic world all add up quickly. For State universities today, these costs could amount to an annual average of more than $30,000. Such a long list of expenses is realistic to consider, it seems to me. Often, universities will quote lower university costs to simplify their estimates because they exclude important expenses such as those mentioned here.

Taking that annual estimate, four years of a State university could easily reach the sum of $120,000 or more per child. In private or ivy league universities those expenses could double or triple.

CAPITAL WE SHOULD ACCUMULATE FOR A CHILD'S HIGHER EDUCATION

Once we determine how much a child's higher education will cost, be it at a community, university or graduate school, it is necessary to know how much we must save monthly to finance these expenses. It is also necessary to bear in mind that university expenses normally are financed with a combination of family savings, financial aid from the public and private sectors, student work and other sources including scholarships.

To give you an idea of how much you should save to fully finance the higher education of your child in a university of the State where you reside, I have prepared the following calculation:

Assumptions:

- Annual average cost of $30,000, for four years, including all expenses of living.

- You start saving when your child is born.

- Your child will enter college at age 18.

- University costs will grow at the same rate of return on investment of education funds, that is, close to 7% per year.
- Calculations are expressed in today's dollars.
- When the child enters the university at 18 years of age the fund has the sum of money necessary to finance the four years.
- Given the calculations and assumptions above, you would have to save $6,667 annually or $556 monthly over the 18 years.

Do not be scared by these figures. It is very possible that between 50 and 75% of this cost could be absorbed by the reduction of some costs by the university to qualified students. This could be through scholarships of various types and amounts, student loans, work-study programs or student work.

An important recommendation is that you ask the financial officer/career advisor at your child's high school, or at the local community college or State university where your child may go, to do basic calculations of university costs. From this, you can begin to estimate how much you should save monthly to finance all or part of these expenses, explore financial aid that could be obtained, and examine higher education alternatives inside and outside the State. Those calculations could decrease or increase the amount you should save over 18 years. At least you will know the options available and most feasible for your situation and goals of your son-daughter.

On the internet there are several websites to help you make these calculations. The website of the US Department of Education gives you significant information about financial aid and how to calculate costs. (www.ed.gov)

DISCUSS WITH CHILDREN THE FINANCING OPTIONS FOR HIGHER EDUCATION

It should be kept in mind that family plans for higher education of the children should not be written in stone but need to be flexible. These plans may need to be modified in line with the family's financial situation over the course of those first 18 years of the child's life. It is possible that they may be able to start in the initial years by depositing only small sums in an Educational Fund but increase them over time.

One planning option for the family is to commit to finance up to 100% of the higher education of their children if they choose a public State university where they reside (Plan A). In this option, parents and the child may also apply for financial aid, allowing them to stretch farther the savings they have accumulated. This is the cost option I find most economical for a four-year program (bachelor's degree), especially if the son/daughter can live at home. If your child performs well at the bachelor's level, he/she may have opportunities to do a master's/doctor's degree at a more costly university, financed in large part with financial aid.

Another planning option may be for the parents to set a different financing goal (Plan B), for example, to commit to financing up to 50% of the cost of an out-of-state university or a private institution or some combination that is financially feasible for the family. The difference could be financed by other means: public and private financial aid, work of the children, specific donations, etc.

Another alternative could be to set a lower goal (Plan C) in which the parents aim to finance a two-year career at a community or technical school. This would leave the children with the responsibility to cover the two years remaining for the university bachelor's degree through working, obtaining financial aid and educational loans, etc.

What must be seriously considered is to assure your children that the family will do everything possible to help finance their higher education. This assurance has to be in line with the real economic possibilities of the family, plus financial help where needed. Keep in mind that the public and private sectors are very generous in this sense, but it takes a lot of research and work to obtain such aid. Above all, it is essential that the student work hard in high school to obtain the best academic record possible and strive for extra-curricular achievements such as in sports, music, science, or community service in order to have a strong application for financial aid.

BENEFITS OF HIGHER EDUCATION

The economic crisis that began in 2007 highlighted in a dramatic way the benefits of higher education not only for future students but also for many parents who had to return to the university or technical colleges to update or acquire new specialties.

Statistics show that the salaries and benefits of those with higher education are greater than for those without that education. This is obvious, but it is worth emphasizing again here because many to easily forget. As in the rest of the world, this society is based on the work ethic that those with university or technical degrees will have better salaries and benefits, better opportunities in the labor force as well as in the social and political world and more possibilities to accumulate capital (a house, equipment, vehicles, financial assets, company stock, etc.).

There are also intangible benefits that come from higher education. It may lead to greater intellectual capacity and maturity to appreciate and be active in the world around them, whether as a citizen, resident, professional, technical specialist, family member, supporter of the environment or other social cause, community volunteer, company employee, or self-employed person. Statistics show that there are fewer people with higher education in prisons than without. This does not mean that the more educated people are better overall. They also may end up with serious moral and legal deficiencies as has been demonstrated in economic crises, particularly the recent one in the 2000s where we still are hearing about major cases of fraud, theft and other abuses in the financial world from that time. Many corporate executives have ended up in jail.

FINANCING

We will now explore how to finance higher education expenses. Generally, financial support comes from a mix of these different sources:

1. Family savings

2. Financial assistance from the public and private sectors

3. Other forms of financing

In practice, university studies commonly are financed with resources from all the means a family can find. This often includes donations from relatives, the parents taking on a second job, part-time work by the student, sale of used things, and other ways to raise money through special activities. The various financial resources are elaborated below.

1. FAMILY SAVINGS

It is important to repeat here that the higher education of the children will most likely be financed, at least in part, by the savings of the family. Financial aid should be considered as supplementary financing. No one knows in the beginning how the child will perform as a student.

The golden rule is to consider that better academic degrees, excellent extra-curricular performance and participation in community activities will be fundamental requirements to obtain adequate financial aid. Even so, families will need to finance at least those expenses that are not normally considered in the calculation of university costs but are necessary to live as a student – mainly housing, food, transportation. For this reason, it is important to consider family saving for higher education of the children an important priority in family financial planning.

2. FINANCIAL ASSISTANCE FROM THE PUBLIC AND PRIVATE SECTOR

To help finance higher education, the US Congress has approved something called "529 plans or accounts" because they are provided in section 529 of the United States tax code. These accounts are sponsored by the States and their government agencies as well as by institutions of higher education. The objective is to help finance university "Qualified Tuition Plans" (QTPs). Each State establishes this type of account according to its own requirements and needs.

The 529 plans are of two types:

- Educational savings account, also known as educational plan 529.

- Advance payment of university studies (prepaid 529 plan).

EDUCATIONAL SAVING ACCOUNT (529 Plan)

The Educational Plan 529 is described in detail here because it is the form of savings for university education that is most used by families. This may be in part because it offers more options for benefits and financing than the prepaid university type plan that we will discuss later.

We must begin by emphasizing that it is important for a couple to include a child's future higher education expenses in its savings planning as soon as possible. Ideally this should be before the child's birth or immediately after. It is best to consider these expenses as long-term investments in the economic and social future of the child.

The time factor is crucial in one's strategy for financing these expenses. Financial calculations on what will be needed should assume that the child will enter the university at age 18. The more time available to save, the greater the capitalization since one can assume the Educational Fund will grow at a compound interest rate between 7% and 10% per year.

The financial and tax advantages of these accounts are greater the more years that the deposits are made, with growth being tax-free. If begun at a child's birth, the parents will have 18 years to build up the education fund. This could be challenging because the couple probably is starting out with other basic expenses at the beginning of their marriage, and they may have relatively low-income levels as they begin their professional or technical careers. Sometimes parents cannot start saving until their children are 5 years old or older. Or they can only do it for no more than one child. Or they simply do not make savings thinking that they would fund higher education expenses with scholarships and other financial aid. Or they will let their children look for ways to pay for their university studies.

Below, I present information on how these accounts function. It is important that you seek more detailed information on this through the internet and the financial offices of educational institutions about how to start this process. In general, 529 accounts or plans have the following characteristics:

- They are sponsored by the States which then establish the respective regulations.
- They are created by a person (owner of the account) for the benefit of a student (beneficiary).
- They may be created by parents, grandparents, relatives, friends or any other person interested in contributing to that account.
- The beneficiaries can be children, grandchildren, nephews, godchildren, children of friends, and even the same parents who open the account.
- The beneficiaries may be residents of another State.
- The beneficiaries can attend public or private universities located in States other than the one in which they reside.
- Students must attend university at least half-time.
- A person can open accounts for different beneficiaries.
- One may change the beneficiaries so long as within the family, for example, changing the beneficiary to someone who qualifies as a sister or cousin in the first grade.
- All contributions to this account must be made in cash or checks.

- You can transfer funds from a 529 account of one State to a similar account in another State once a year without incurring penalties.

Qualifying universities. The universities that can participate in these plans are those that are accredited by the Department of Education of the respective State. They include institutions that offer associate degrees (2 years), baccalaureate (4 years), masters, doctorates, professional and technical degrees and other training and specialized studies after having obtained a high school diploma.

Opening an account. To open the account, one may go directly to any of the financial institutions with which the State maintains contracts for the 529 plan administration. This includes such firms as Merrill Lynch, Fidelity Investments, John Hancock, Charles Schwab, T. Rowe Price and some Trust Funds established by the States or universities.

Another way to open an account is to go to an authorized broker who sells 529 plans. I think that this alternative is usually more expensive. You have to pay for the broker's services in addition to any other sales commissions that may be charged when using one of the financial institutions mentioned above.

It is important to keep in mind that Education Savings 529 accounts are considered assets of the owner(s) of the account. This can affect the calculation of "financial need" of the student, increasing the value of the "expected contribution of the family" and decreasing the financial need of the student from other financial aid sources.

Contributions. Contributions can be made automatically from a checking or savings account or through the personnel office where you work if you ask them to deduct a monthly amount from your salary and deposit it into this account. There is no limit to contribute to these plans. The minimum limit to get started is very low, often less than $ 100. This flexibility allows families to open an account early on according to their means. These deposits are made with dollars that have already paid the federal income tax.

Contributions to these plans generally do not pay State income tax. In some States these contributions are considered an exemption or deduction when calculating the basis on which State taxes to be paid. It is important to get advice from the State tax office knowledgeable about these accounts.

The earnings obtained through the investment of these contributions grow free of tax. This advantage increases the capitalization in these accounts more quickly.

Withdrawal of funds. Owners of the account have the power to control the fund's withdrawals. They can only do so to pay qualified university expenses of the beneficiaries of the account to qualified institutions. The owner(s) control the withdrawal and use of money. This cannot be done by the student beneficiary of the account. The owner(s) of the account can change the beneficiary, but not the destination of the funds. The owners of the account can withdraw money to pay for university studies outside the State where the account is held. This is an important advantage.

Withdrawals of money from the account are not taxed if they are to pay for the universities qualified educational expenses. University expenses that qualify to be financed by these accounts include tuition, fees, books, computers, scientific equipment and certain lodging and food expenses. If the owners of the account withdraw funds for other purposes, they must pay taxes on the investment income related to the withdrawn funds and in addition a 10% penalty on those profits. The 10% fine does not apply if the beneficiary dies, is physically disabled, or acquires a scholarship.

There is a special inheritance tax regime and taxes on donations made by parents or grandparents. Consult the financial officer of the institution where they want to open the account if they wish to use this feature. This tax exemption is very generous and can be a great solution to finance the university studies of children or grandchildren.

Investment of funds. The investment of contributions/deposits is made by the State through the financial institutions with which it has contracts to professionally manage these accounts. The owners of the accounts can choose from among several investment plans that are offered by financial institutions. Once a plan is chosen it must stay in the plan for at least one year before switching to another. An important factor to consider is that the owners of the account cannot participate in decisions about how to invest these funds. They can only choose the type of fund and its structure once a year.

Expenses associated with Education Savings 529 Plan. It must be understood that these plans have several expenses. Of course, there are the costs charged by the mutual funds that are included in the investment options offered by the financial administrators of these accounts. In addition, there are other expenses. These include a charge for establishing the account, annual cost of maintaining the account and expenses for financially managing the assets of the account. There are distinct charges also to transfer the account to another account, charges for individual financial transactions, and costs of sale when the plans are purchased directly from an intermediary or broker. It is important to be well-informed about these costs because the different investment options may have different charges.

Recommendations. When considering opening an Education Savings 529 Plan, begin by researching the tax, financial and flexibility benefits offered by the 529 Plan in the State where you reside. Then ask the financial officer who is helping you to explain the same in a comparative way with other States that your child is considering. Currently there are many families who choose to open their 529 accounts in other States because of the better investment opportunities they offer and more friendly regulations for beneficiaries.

Among the factors to consider when deciding to open a 529 account of this type are the following: the various investment plans offered and the total and detailed costs of managing these accounts. This latter factor is particularly important since there is a great variety of costs, fees, commissions, etc., (as noted above) which are difficult to envision. Also, it is important to understand the regulations and restrictions that the 529 account has in the chosen State, the residency requirements and other conditions that you should analyze with the financial officer. Remember these aspects vary, sometimes significantly, from State to State.

UNIVERSITY PREPAID TUITIONS PLANS

This type of 529 plan allows parents to pay the current costs for the university that their children will attend in the future. Parents can pre-purchase a certain number of credits or other units of study at current prices.

The objective is to avoid the inflation of these expenses which is usually much higher than the consumer price index. By making these advance arrangements, parents seek cost savings for inflation and other savings that may be negotiated with the university. For instance, in most cases, accommodation and food expenses are not included, but there are some universities that do include them. A variety of other expenses (transportation, communications, insurance, clothing, etc.) are not included, so it is up to the family to see how to finance them.

These plans are sponsored by State governments and have local residency requirements. Many universities also sponsor this type of plan. An important advantage is that many States guarantee the investments in these prepaid plans.

There are also restrictions or requirements such as the following:

- The student is required to go to the university that has been pre-paid.

- It is possible that the student does not meet the requirements to be admitted to that university.

- The student has limited choice to choose the university he/she wants to attend.

- The student could receive a scholarship to attend that or another university.

- The student does not qualify or decides not to go to the university with the pre-paid plan.

It is also important to consider that universities have different plans for advance payments. So the family should investigate all options in detail. It is key to get advice from specialists in higher education financing whether they may be in high school or university offices or working as an independent financial planner.

Another factor to consider is that savings accounts in general may give better economic return over the time involved. Savings accounts also generally have more flexibility when it comes to selecting the university, being able to wait until the student is ready, and not have to lock into one university with a pre-paid plan when the child is still an infant.

3. OTHER FORMS OF FINANCING

Other sources of funding for higher education include grants, scholarships and loans. The economic crisis at the end of 2007 made grants one of the most important forms of financing not only for students but also for higher education institutions because they received the funds for the studies provided. Grants include free financial aid (scholarships to cover part or all of the cost), university low-interest loans, and university work-study programs (reduced tuition). Our society is very generous in providing this type of help. It can come from multiple sources:

- Free financial aid from the federal, state or local government
- Student loans from the public and private sectors
- Financial aid from non-profit organizations
- Free financial help from corporations, including scholarships
- Grants from dedicated education funds or foundations

The society in general and the institutions of the public and private sectors recognize that the economic, social and cultural development of the country depends on and is a reflection of the quality of its inhabitants, our human infrastructure. The quality of life and economic security of the inhabitants depends on the education and training they have acquired during their formative years (first 25 years) and on the work, professional and business experience they have gained during their productive years (25 to 65 years).

This mean that large amounts of resources are allocated by a wide variety of diverse institutions in order to give an opportunity to any person who is determined to pursue higher-level studies and finish them successfully. Economists consider that educational support is not an expense but an investment in the country's future because it creates human capital capable of producing social and economic benefits that have a value much higher than the higher educational costs.

A higher education generally brings with it the potential for higher income, more job security and the possibility of obtaining economic independence and reaching financial goals for retirement at the desired age. Forecasts for meaningful employment, good salaries and benefits in the 21st century are in direct relation to the academic and technical capacity of individuals as well as their training and experience. Competition in this century for well-paid jobs will increasingly come from national as well as global and international markets where there are hundreds of millions of potential workers. By the middle of this century, the world population is expected to be almost 10 9 billion.

A main message to remember from this chapter is that a wide and diverse array of financial resources are available to those who can meet certain requirements based on academic record, financial capacity and need, and other accomplishments in such activities as sports, music, the arts, community service, or military service. Financial resources are accessible to all those who aspire to higher education, work hard both academically and to find appropriate financial aid toward this end, and be dedicated and serious throughout this endeavor.

One needs to appreciate that qualified students with more economic need typically will have priority for aid. This does not mean that those with a better economic situation are prevented from obtaining needed resources. Institutions that award financial aid assistance consider also other factors such as family size, number of children and other dependents, how many children are in college, high family medical expenses or the overall cost of the university they wish to attend, which may be higher than some others.

HOW MUCH FINANCIAL AID IS NEEDED?

This question is essential to understand and address because the answer greatly affects your chances of getting financial help. The vast majority of institutions that offer financial aid require that the student's financial need be determined as accurately as possible. In the case of the Federal government, the following procedure applies:

1. Obtain the forms to request financial assistance. These forms (called FAFSA for "Free Application for Federal Student Aid") can be obtained in the offices of your child's high school, the U.S. Department of Education or the offices of the community college or university your child wants to attend. It is very important to be well informed about the information requested, deadlines for submission, and where to get help in case they are difficult to fill out personally. The ideal for you is to obtain them with enough advance time to start collecting the information requested with calm and avoid last-minute panic.

2. The completed FAFSA forms are sent to the university you want to attend. Offices there assess the financial need of the student and their family. The university may require additional information on its own forms.

3. To make the financial evaluation, the university uses a formula provided by the U.S. Congress called Expected Fam-

ily Contribution (EFC). This is used to determine how many resources the family can contribute to finance the higher education of the applicant. Various family factors are considered, including income, wages and other compensation, investments, accumulated assets such as property, inventories of goods, retirement funds, unemployment payments, social security income, and debts. Other factors also considered include the number of dependent children in the family, how many are in the university or finishing high school, medical debts, years before the parents can retire.

4. Financial aid is calculated by subtracting the family's expected contribution from the cost of the university studies. To be eligible for financial aid there are also other requirements. These include whether the university will be attended full-time, half-year or only part-time. Of course, the academic results of previous years are also considered.

5. If the cost of the university is equal to or less than the expected contribution of the family, it is possible there may be no financial aid offered because family resources are sufficient. Or the result may be that the family situation allows contributing not all but a certain percentage of the costs. For example, let's say the university cost of Marta Julia's second year of her 4-year study program is $30,000; if the calculations indicate the family can contribute 40% of the university cost that would make their responsibility $12,000. Whether financial aid is available ultimately depends on the type of university and its costs because the expected contribution of the family is more or less fixed while the cost of the university will vary by university, for example, whether it is in-state or out-of-state, public or private, large or small, looking for more students or over-booked, ivy-league, etc. On the internet you can get more information about these calculations (see: studentaid.ed.gov),

6. Some factors may substantially reduce the Expected Financial Contribution (or EFC) needed by the family. These include a student over 23 years old, or married, or in a master's or doctorate program, or a military veteran, or an orphan until age 18, or with dependents not from his wife. In such cases, the applicant is declared an independent student, which substantially reduces the expected contribution of the family. Any one of these factors is sufficient for the applicant to be declared an independent student. This reduction in the EFC increases the amount of financial assistance one can request from the Federal government.

7. To summarize key points, remember that tax advantages, amount of flexibility in choice of university, independence of decision-making on fund investment, withdrawal of funds, limitations, fines and other requirements will vary between these two types of 529 plans. It is important to be advised by the financial aid specialists in order to choose the one that best suits the interests and needs of the family. A tax advisor also can give you valuable advice on how to minimize 529 Plan expenses.

8. In light of the above, my advice is to start as soon as possible to gather needed information, be honest in determining your financial status and need, complete and submit the necessary forms, making sure all the questions are answered completely and as best possible. And, always stay informed through the internet of the options available and get advice from the financial aid advisors of the child's high school and university of interest. These specialists also can review your financial aid application before you send it in. Keep a copy of all the information you gather and submit and any additional requests they send. A good filing cabinet and filing system can help you manage this information efficiently.

9. And remember: a family that is informed and seriously plans ahead can greatly reduce the direct family expenses of higher education for their children. The existing programs are numerous and generous. Many of these are complementary, meaning that several can be applied for and used simultaneously from public, private, non-profit, or international sources.

EDUCATIONAL SAVINGS SYSTEMS WITH TAX ADVANTAGES

The same section 529 of the US Tax Code offers the Educational Savings Account "COVERDELL", which is similar to an IRA with a limitation of contributions and income of the contributor. There are other systems created by other provisions of the Tax Code that offer tax advantages such as the ROTH and IRA savings accounts normally used as retirement funds but which can also be used for financing university studies.

Other programs that offer tax advantages could be explored to help finance higher education. One is the HOPE (Helping Others Pursue Education) Program which provides scholarships and grants for degree studies with tax reductions for bachelors, masters, doctorate and specialization courses. There also are Series EE and I Bonds issued after 1989, where the bond owner pays qualified higher education expenses at an eligible institution. There also may be some exclusion, deduction or credit for interest paid for educational loans, as well as special tax treatment for higher education expenses paid by an employer. Some qualified higher education expenses may be able to be excluded from the gross income of a person or family, including interest payments on lines of credit based on real estate custody accounts (home equity loans) taken out for the education benefit of a child.

TYPES OF FINANCIAL AID FROM THE FEDERAL GOVERNMENT

The US Department of Education offers several types of scholarships (grants) and educational loans. The two best-known scholarships are the following: the Federal PELL scholarships (for students with financial need, who have not earned their first bachelor's degree, or who are enrolled in certain post-baccalaureate programs, through participating institutions, at: https://studentaid.ed.gov/sa/types/grants-scholarships/pell) and the FESOGP (Federal Educational Supplemental Opportunity Grant Program), a grant to undergraduate students with exceptional need (see https://studentaid.ed.gov/sa/types/grants-scholarships/fseog). Among the loans available, the following can be mentioned: Stafford, PLUS, and Consolidation Loans. Other federal financial aid includes the Federal Work-study program and Federal Perkins loans.

Each of these financing programs has its own characteristics and requirements. It is important to get advice from financial aid officers at a nearby high school or college to determine which one, if any, suits your family situation. I recommend that you do research on these programs through the internet before having such a meeting. There is a lot of information available.

OTHER FINANCIAL AID

The Departments of Education at the State level have financial aid programs similar to those of the Federal government. The States use the same calculations to determine the student's financial need but add other requirements. These include having a good academic record in the past, residing in the State where the application is being submitted and attending a university in that State.

Universities also have their own financial aid programs which could include scholarships, loans, discounts on tuition, and job offers at the university. Other factors that may have weight, depending on the university, include excellent academic record or special achievements in sports, the arts, science, or music.

The US Armed Forces have financial aid programs for their members. The best ways to learn about these programs is, first, through the internet and, second, making a visit to the recruiting or personnel offices of the respective institutions.

Civic and non-profit organizations also offer a variety of grants, particularly scholarships or donations based on the student's financial need, academic background, and affiliation to that institution. Among these to mention are the Boys/Girls Scouts, American Legion, Rotary Club, YMCA, Community Foundations, and Chambers of Commerce. Churches and religious institutions (e.g., Knights of Columbus, Jewish Community organizations) also may have a grants program for students seeking help with higher education costs. This type of help should be investigated, first, through the internet and, second, through contact with the specific institution of interest, if feasible. Such effort is more labor-intensive because there are many diverse institutions, but it is worth it.

We must be reminded, again, that the most common scholarships and grants normally do not offer help for accommodation, food and other basic living expenses. However, this aid does not require repayment. There is a broader type of scholarship that includes accommodation, food and other basic needs, along with tuition and other academic expenses. These are sometimes referred to as 'fellowships' for post-graduate studies, masters and doctorates, and in some undergraduate cases, the university covers all costs including a stipend for living expenses.

OTHER FORMS OF FINANCING

Another financing option is to obtain a loan from your 401k account. You may request a loan against this account for your child's higher education up to $50,000. You pay back the loan at a lower rate than the market rate over a period of five years. Do not forget that these funds are your savings for retirement. If you lose your job you have only 90 days to pay the entire loan. If you do not, you must pay a 10% fine and income taxes on the amount withdrawn if you are under 59 ½ years old. Also, keep in mind that while such a loan increases family income, it also decreases your child's eligibility for financial aid from other sources.

Possibilities for using your social security also may exist. If you turn 62, you have the right to receive social security payments (a pension) up to 80% of what you would be entitled to if you had waited until age 66 and received a full pension. From the age of 62 you can also receive payments equivalent to half of your pension for each child under 18 who is in primary or secondary school. The maximum that you may receive for this benefit is 180% of your pension.

As another option, one member of a married couple can choose to retire at age 62 and access payments for their children of school age. The other member may continue working until age 66 and receive the full pension. A further option is for both to wait until age 66 and receive full pensions which they can then suspend until age 70. However, the children may be able to receive a pension equivalent to 50% of that of one of their parents once that parent files for the full pension at age 66 even though it is then suspended.

RECOMMENDATIONS AND COMMENTS

1. Establish an Educational Savings Plan 529 as soon as feasible

I recommend that when a child is born into your family, you proceed to open some type of Education Fund such as the Educational Savings Plan 529 (discussed above) even if you can deposit only $50. This can also provide the basis for a campaign to encourage grandparents, uncles, godparents, intimate friends, and patrons to make contributions to this account on birthdays, end of the year parties, the day of the saints, other special days. An envelope with some money for this account will be appreciated immediately by the parents and with time by the child. It is very easy to do, so it would be a pity if the parents, godparents or grandparents not to take the opportunity.

I recommend opening an Educational Savings 529 Plan for each child because it is the most common, there is a lot of family experience managing this type of account because it is similar to the IRA, and there are many qualified financial institutions throughout the country available to help. In relation to how they are opened, where and other details, I recommend you go to some financial institution that commonly handles financial aid programs for students such as Fidelity, Charles Schwab, or Merrill Lynch. They will help you fill out the forms and make the first deposit. They will also give you detailed information on how to manage the account, its conditions, and costs.

2. Other tasks for parents

It is essential, as a first step, for parents to envision and plan for their children going to a 4-year university, 2-year community college, or other technical school when they leave high school. This can be a goal to instill in their children and parents have 18 years to do it.

To support this assumption, parents need to start by asking themselves some questions. What happens if they do nothing to help finance the higher education of their children? What will be their future throughout this century if they do not have enough education, training, and experience to compete?

As a second step, parents should open an Education Fund, such as a 529 plan type account as I suggested at the beginning and start a campaign to deposit money in it. You can only make contributions in cash or checks in this type of accounts. The investment of these funds is made automatically by the financial institution managing the account.

Undoubtedly, there are many alternatives for setting up an Education Fund. That decision depends on many factors unique to the family—number of children, family economic conditions presently and projected for the future, family stability (divorce?), academic and social achievements of the child, opportunities for student work together with study, potential offers of financing from different sources, etc. Hence there is a need, as part of the funding plan, for parents to build in some flexibility.

Flexibility is necessary. But as parents you still need to set some minimum goals by which you can help with financing. That minimum, based on cost calculations and family capacity to help, ideally is a promise to finance at least the 2-year community college associates degree (probably living at home) or an equivalent of 50% of the local 4-year university for a bachelor's degree (again living at home). Then, if your financial situation improves or if financial aid is generous, the situation may improve.

3. Involve your children – establish some ground rules

It is important to involve the children in these tasks in order to instill a clear sense of the sacrifices, costs, and benefits of pursuing such studies. In addition, they will learn early on the complexities of the bureaucratic world and how to manage in that environment.

Critical in this process is the need for the parents and children to establish together some principles or rules that will apply to the possibilities for family financing. When the children are starting high school, it is important to begin talking talk with them about the higher education options available, parents' ability to help with finance, and what is expected of the children in terms of grades and achievements in high school and then in college.

One point to stress is that the children may apply to all the universities they want, even the most prestigious and expensive, recognizing that each has an application fee they must cover. This will help them freely explore what is available for any type of study and the entrance requirements. It will also give them information about costs so that they can visualize forms of financing (family, financial aid, loans, personal work and others) for each option they analyze.

Parents can decide to discourage or eliminate the option of getting a student loan to finance their studies. Parents can limit funding only to family savings, scholarships, and student work. This may establish a reasonable cost ceiling for the student. If the chosen university is beyond that ceiling, the student should simply eliminate it from the list, pure and simple. There is always the possibility for the student to go to a prestigious university for postgraduate studies (masters and doctorates) where there may be more scholarships and the possibility for the student to finance the difference with their own work. It is assumed that he/she will obtain better income and more stability at studies and work once one has a bachelor's degree.

An alternative option for parents is to commit to funding four years but only at the state university where they reside. If the student does not finish in that period (except for very qualified exceptions) he/she will need to find other financing for the extra time needed to finish.

Parents can make certain additional demands, especially related to high performance, summer internships where they can learn good work habits (schedules, discipline, personal appearance, etc.), and interaction with professionals in their field and to begin to practice their discipline. This will help give a sense of what is possible with what they will do once they graduate, hopefully when they are paid much better.

Finally, as an added personal incentive for students to achieve excellence in their studies, parents may promise prizes such as financing part of a car, buying certain electronic equipment, a trip abroad, or other incentive, if feasible.

4. Do everything possible to obtain financial aid

Another important task is to learn about the various financial aids that may be available and how to take advantage of them in a timely fashion. Ask your children to talk with the financial advisor at their high school to get all the information they can and to make an appointment for parents and children to meet with the advisor together.

It is important to be informed of all financial aid programs that might be available: federal, state, colleges, institutes, universities, corporations, non-profit organizations and others. Study well the requirements, forms, processes, costs, and conditions linked to these programs.

A financial planner can be very helpful here because not only will he/she advise you about these programs and their expenses, but he/she may be able to assess the financial situation of the family for what it can contribute. Ideally, a couple should consult a financial planner when they begin their family life in order to benefit from an overview of family finances, goals, and planning to achieve those goals.

5. Student loans – be careful and cautious

Without a clear and justified reason, do not endorse or co-sign for a student loan. Remember your retirement. If your child or other beneficiary of your co-signed loan does not pay what is owed either monthly or for the full balance in a timely fashion, you are responsible to pay. If you do not pay (for whatever reason), that debt will affect your credit report and make future borrowing more expensive as well as risk your personal reputation. And you will have a stressed relationship with those whom you benefited with your goodwill. And do not forget that the loan will have to be paid in time even if your child becomes disabled or dies. Likewise, student loans are not included in bankruptcy statements and will continue to be active debts until paid.

Another important factor to consider is how the loan monies are going to be made available. The bank may authorize a checking account with a debit card, to which amounts can be withdrawn which are considered to be a loan. Or the loan may be in the form of a prepaid Bank card. The cost of using that money in either case may be high for all fees and commissions charged or fines if payments are delinquent.

Student loans and the associated fees and fines have become an important source of income for banks, financial institutions and universities. The loans are often in the form of credit or debit cards with all the costs already charged. Today there are student loans of this nature of more than one trillion dollars, more than the total of all other forms of credit card debt.

The worst thing that can happen to a student striving to get a higher education is to get into debt for a while and then decide not to continue studying. In this case he/she is left without a university or technical-professional degree and with a large debt. This situation can affect other important decisions of one's life, such as when to marry, when to have children, possibilities for buying a house, etc.

An additional problem with taking on a student loan, is that many students fall behind in making the required repayments once they are out of school and start having income. This delinquency affects their credit report (with serious implications for other financial aspects in their life) and increases their total debt because interest not paid is added to the debt. principal.

One-way students can defend themselves from large student debt is by moving from an expensive private or out-of-state university to one to their state of residence or a local community college where costs are much cheaper. That move also could include more financial help to cover almost all study expenses. The aim is to find ways to get an education while avoiding loans or not continuing to borrow.

A revealing article about the big financial business of student loans was recently published in regional and national newspapers. Written by Daniel Wagner (Business reporter), the article reveals the huge profits that banks and financial institutions make from contracts with universities to deliver financial aid to the students. The way this happens is by delivering financial aid through debit cards linked to a bank current account or prepaid cards on which it is possible to charge a variety of commissions, fees, fines and other charges. The article mentions that some financial institutions are charging as many as 12 different fees.

Particularly unfortunate with student loans, especially through the use debit or prepaid cards, is the fact that they leave the students, especially those just starting, exposed to aggressive advertising campaigns that promote the use of these cards. Keep in mind that most students have very little experience managing their personal finances. Temptations are enormous when a young person finds himself/herself with money that is available and solely under his/her control.

As for the receiving institutions, using debit or prepaid cards simplifies the administrative work of the university and intermediary financial institutions as it substantially reduces their processing costs. They do not need officials to process account statements and payment slips, make check deposits, keep records, or offices and equipment to do this, and save in telephone and other communication services. Their offices can have a minimum of staff and computers to process and do follow-ups. Unfortunately, these savings commonly are not transferred to the students who are beneficiaries of such loans and grants.

THE INCOME STRATEGY

Let's start by remembering the basic formula of family finances to help make sense of the economic concept of income:

INCOME = CONSUMPTION EXPENSES + SAVINGS AND INVESTMENTS

The income received by a person or family for any purpose is used to buy the goods and services needed to sustain daily life and what is left is used for savings and investment.

We cannot spend more than we receive. If we do, we get into debt. Debt means we must pay the installments of loans with our income. If we do not pay, we fall into bankruptcy, which causes serious economic risk and psychological damage. The uncontrolled use of credit cards and personal loans gives us the illusion of being at a level of income and consumption that does not correspond to our long-term capacity. What we are doing in that situation is consuming the income that we will receive in the future, but with a high cost in the form of interest, commissions and fines.

WHAT DOES IT MEAN TO BE ECONOMICALLY INDEPENDENT?

The wisest thing that a couple can do is to achieve *as soon as possible enough capital in a pension account to generate an income stream that allows them a satisfactory life after a certain age without worries.*

I always refer to the financial needs of a family of four, two adults with two children. I assume that the two adults work and share their incomes. The general rule is that the retirement is done about 65 years of age, but we know that some people achieve economic independence before, some during the decade of their 50s.

For this latter group, retirement does not mean that when one achieves financial independence, he/she goes home and does nothing. On the contrary, what it means is that they now have the freedom to choose what to do with their lives from then on. This may mean to keep working, change activities, study, do volunteer work, write, travel, help your family, become a small business person etc.

Typically, people continue to work until they reach retirement age or beyond if necessary, for the income. Some may have achieved economic independence earlier but decided to continue working for a variety of reasons: satisfaction with work, good salary and benefits, lack of other options, maintaining social ties, avoiding loneliness, etc. Others may be forced to continue working because they started late to save enough for what they now need or are saturated with debt.

The problem is to define what is the minimum income. For many, according to experts, this minimum is roughly equivalent to 80% of the average annual income of the last three years of their working life. For others, only 70% of that income could be enough. If the couple has their house paid, with no debts, the children living independently outside the house and is in good health, the minimum may even be a lower percentage. In the end, it must be an amount that allows one to live in what can be consider an acceptable retirement.

WHY INCREASE OUR INCOME?

It is important to try to increase your income because it is one of the most intelligent things a person can do in the 21st century.

More income allows you to increase your *saving and investing.* Remember that labor income growth at 2 to 3% a year, more or less with the inflation rate. From 1970 that has been the salary increases in nominal term. If you discount the inflation from the salaries, they have been stagnant or sometimes negatives during that period.

Investment, on their part, has been historically growing at 8 to 10% a year in a compound way. The combined impact of interest rate, longtime saving and investing, compounding effect and the deferred taxes make your savings grow much higher and faster. So, the more income the more saving possibilities to grow at higher rate of returns. See the table below for those effects on savings of 10% invested at 6% and 7% for 30 or 40 years.

ANNUAL RETURNS OF INVESTED FUNDS

ANNUAL INCOME	ANNUAL SAVING 10%	RETURNS 6% 30 YEARS	RETURNS 7% 30 YEARS	RETURNS 6% 40 YEARS	RETURNS 7% 40 YEARS
$ 50,000	$ 5,000	$ 395,290	$ 472,304	$ 773,810	$ 998,176
$ 60,000	$ 6,000	$ 474,349	$ 566,765	$ 928,572	$ 1,197,811
$ 70,000	$ 7,000	$ 553,407	$ 661,226	$ 1,083,334	$ 1,397,446
$ 80,000	$ 8,000	$ 632,465	$ 755,686	$ 1,238,096	$ 1,597,081
$ 90,000	$ 9,000	$ 711,523	$ 850,147	$ 1,392,858	$ 1,797,716
$ 100,000	$ 10,000	$ 790,582	$ 944,608	$ 1,547,620	$ 1,966,351

The changes taking place in the global labor markets are demanding increasingly qualified workers with relevant experience and knowledge. This new type of worker will have access to better salary, benefits, and job security. You must always think about the possibility that you may need to be repositioning yourself at some point in your working life to stay as a qualified, innovating and achieving worker.

It is always possible to achieve better salaries and benefits. There are several ways of doing it: acquiring the *habit* of study and permanent training in the most modern and relevant sectors of the economy, learning from work experience, developing a good attitude or willingness to work with excellence along with staying in good health.

Your responsibility is to obtain the maximum you can in compensation and benefits given the new working conditions. You cannot remain stuck at one level throughout your entire life. You must progress. This is the only way to defend yourself economically in these changing times.

Increasing one's income has become a permanent need and challenge. Higher income means that somebody is rewarding us for well-done jobs. It is a recognition of our contribution to the institution in which we work and by extension as a contribution to our family, community and society in general.

HOW TO GET GREATER INCOME

One way to get greater income is through good job performance and promotions to more higher positions, bonuses, awards and grade increases.

Another way is to have the opportunity to make a lateral transfer up to a job in your same company or to another area where you can perform well. In some cases, this may mean a change to another geographical area or country. Depending on your personal station these may provide good opportunities to learn about other aspects of your company and position yourself better for future promotions.

Another option is to get a job in another company that offers better salaries, benefits and promotions. All future opportunities depend on the trail you left in your previous job, work output and personal behavior in your duties. This is your working capital, your labor value which allows you to move vertical and horizontally in the labor market.

Another way occurs when one member of the couple who was not working decides to get a job. Today, it is rare that a spouse does not work. This commonly occurs when one of the spouses stays home to care for and educate their children. Once this obligation is met, the spouse returns to the labor market. All the calculations and recommendations made in this book assume that both members of a couple work and thus there are two incomes.

An additional option occurs when one of the spouses decides to get a second job. This is recommended in certain circumstances, for example:

- To save extra for the "down payment" for a car or for a mortgage.

- To reduce accumulated debts on your credit cards and eventually eliminate some cards.

- To accelerate the payment of the mortgage by either refinancing to 15 years or paying the principal more quickly.

- To pay some expenses arising from emergencies.

Another way to generate income may result from work done at home "online". Every day there are more opportunities for this type of work from consultancies, distance education, data processing, sales, accounting, preparation of tax returns, etc.

Having a stable job is an excellent way to generate safe and sufficient income to live well. Obviously, one is obliged to live within the limits of those salaries and benefits. Keep in mind that the benefits sometimes almost double the wages. As noted above a well-qualified person with good job performance can expand that income through promotions, bonuses or other incentives.

It is important to note, however, that not everyone has the vocation to be employed by somebody else and to depend almost exclusively on a salary, benefits and the will of an employer. Likewise, not everyone has the education and training enough to become employees of a major corporation, government or non-governmental institution.

A business friend who has a small business told me once that he regretted not having studied something because if he had he could have gotten a job with a better salary than the profits in his business. In a regular job, he reflected, one arrives at eight or nine in the morning and leaves at five or six in the afternoon without major worries. If you are self-employed you must be working every day of the year, without a schedule, paying all your own benefits[6], assuming all risks and being always worried about the future.

Some people may feel satisfied with the level of income they produce. The work in the corporation or in the government may seem safe, the salary sufficient, their work well accepted. They may have

6. The self-employed pay the Social Security and Medicare taxes twice as employee and employer, that is 15.3% of gross salary.

no relationship problems with their boss and coworkers, their schedule may be convenient, and their transportation from home to work acceptable. No major economic problems are seen in the future.

Therefore, they see no reason to study more, to try harder or to aspire to greater responsibilities and income. For some, the cost of this attitude in the short or medium term could be stagnation, obsolescence, loss of opportunities and, even, loss of the job you have if it is modernized or moved.

There is always the possibility of improving your potential for generating more income. You may take relevant courses at a community college, university or specialized knowledge institution. You may seek more training at your corporation or government agency to add to the experience gained at work.

You should not forget that you have a virtual money meter (like a taximeter) in your chest. This is the way the employer looks at it. Every hour that passes you should be producing an income that pays your salary and benefits plus covers a part of the company's other costs while still making certain profit. If not, the employer loses money with you. If you are productive, you have an assured future.

FACTORS TO TAKE INTO ACCOUNT TO IMPROVE INCOME.

Whatever the source of income (from an employer or your own small business) the possibility of generating higher income depends on several factors: education, training, experience, work attitude, physical and mental health, age, geographical location, personal circumstances, being objective, being realistic and living in the here and now, having good criteria, common sense and above all the ambition to advance and obtain a higher income.

Self-discipline, meeting schedules, doing things well without supervision, not cheating, being honest, being sober, having a decent personal appearance, respecting people, doing excellent work even giving more than what is require are characteristics of a well-formed person and worker. All of the above open opportunities for promotions and job offers in the labor market.

In this fast-changing world, we will have to continue studying for the rest of our lives and acquiring values that enrich our character. The technical institutes, community colleges and universities should always be present in our plans and activities. Likewise, the programs that develop our character, appearance and attitudes often offered by non-governmental organizations such as churches, personal development centers and other social service institutions.

Remember that today it is not enough to have a high school degree. A degree from a community college helps, but it is not enough. A bachelor's degree (four university years) could be considered today a minimum to aspire to a career with relative security and income. Lately, for many professions it is graduate studies (master's degree) that ensure better income, job availability and social mobility. Naturally, everything depends on your specialty, experience, character.

Everything mentioned above should be considered when making an application either for a new job or moving up in your current company. We also know that applications have more value when they are accompanied by good personal references regarding your character as a person.

In addition, personal contacts are increasingly important. Job literature highlights the importance of networks of personal contacts and friendships. These could be developed through your university, place of employment, professional associations, clients of the company where you work, competing companies, social relations, your trade organization, encounters in sports fields, cultural events and other gatherings.

As one advances in age, it is assumed that a person increases his/her income either by seniority, promotions or new skills. This income growth comes too when the individual is freer of financial obligations: the children may now live independently outside the home; the mortgage is paid, or the amount of the monthly payment is less in proportion to the salary. The home expenditures have diminished as well as the debts. This allows the couple to begin to increase substantially the savings in their pension funds.

But not all couples are in this situation. As discussed above, one of them may be forced to get a second job or both may need to work beyond the age of 65 to increase their pension funds and retire with some financial security. Unfortunately, as of 2017, almost 50% of people over 55 years of age are in this situation.

To give an idea of the importance of growing income throughout one's working life, to build enough retirement funds, below are some projections that I recommend you consider. The most common to begin with is of a person that at age 25 should already have accumulated retirement capital equivalent to 20% of his/her gross salary.

By age 30 years from 30 to 40% of annual gross income

At age 35 years from 160 to 180% of annual gross income.

At age 45 from 300 to 400% of annual gross income.

At age 55 from 800 to 1,000% of annual gross income.

At age 65 from 1,600 to 2,000% (16 to 20 times) of annual gross income.

This means that a person or couple 55 years old with an annual gross income of $80,000 will need to have accumulated and invested in their pension fund at least $640,000 (8 times or 800% of their gross income) and should continue to contribute each year 15% of their gross annual income until they reach age 65, an age at which they could retire with $1,280,000 or $1,600,000.

Finally, it is also interesting to point out the luck factor: being in the right place at the right time. This is especially useful when the person has the credentials and is alert to opportunities around him/her.

REMEMBER: GOOD LUCK DOES NOT COME AUTOMATICALLY IT NEEDS TO BE MADE

In a magazine I recently read an interview with the successful Guatemalan singer-songwriter, Ricardo Arjona. He said: "I believe that we have to walk, move, to discover life, to find things. You carve out your own path in which opportunities appear and that with hard work, tenacity and experience one can transform them into reality."

TRANSFORM YOURSELF INTO AN EFFICIENT ENTREPRENEUR FOR YOUR LIFE

Recognize and act with the conviction that you can always do things better: a process, a product, a sale. Learn by watching carefully, analyzing what you see, taking notes, identifying causes and effects of deviations from our goals. How to correct and improve. Likewise, continue to put more energy in what you do, be more creative, seek to innovate, take advantage of the opportunities offered. The key is to be in a permanent state of alert, exploration, action and improvement. It is about gradually improving in an upward spiral. If you don't do it, you will descend in that spiral.

Learn to do your job well, discover new ways to do it, propose simplifications, modernizations, cost reductions, new designs, new product and sales ideas. Work efficiently, be productive, timely. Develop your own, internal engine. Act as if you were the owner of your own future, because you are.

Try to make your superiors observe and recognize your labor value so that they take it into account in future promotions or increases in wages and benefits. Do not get behind, stay current on the job and promote yourself. Remember that you will sell better in the job market if you have a good backpack of studies, experience in doing creative meaningful work and in solving problems and of course having good references.

Protect yourself from possible dismissal or loss of your job in a period of economic crisis, internal restructuring or sale of the company to another company. The training and education recommendations already mentioned in the previous paragraphs are the best defense you can have.

And unfortunately, if you are unemployed, this is the best time to link to study and training centers. These activities will keep you mentally active, connect you with possible sources of work and prepare you for when the economy comes back. There are many service mechanisms offered by our society, free of charge or at modest cost, to always improve your ability to earn.

THE SPENDING STRATEGY

Everything is connected in our daily lives and everything we do has financial consequences. Let's review again the basic formula of family finances:

INCOME = CONSUMPTION EXPENSES + SAVINGS AND INVESTMENTS

This formula tells us that the income that a person or family receives goes either to buy the goods and services needed to sustain daily life or to savings to deposit in a pension fund and cover other investments (mortgage, automobile, higher education, emergency fund, etc.). There are no other options. This is a law of economics. We cannot spend and save more than we receive.

Even when we get into debt (in other words we expend now our future salaries and other income) to cover the mortgage, car loan, student loan, credit card and other debts, our income must be enough to pay those debts monthly. If it is not enough, we go bankrupt with serious consequences for our individual and family economic futures. Apart from losing what we buy (the physical consequence), we may become psychologically and mentally affected. So here are some golden rules for a basic spending strategy:

GOLDEN RULES

- Save first and consume later.

- Save 15 to 20% of any income you receive automatically.

- The most ambitious do 25% in savings and 75% for house expenditures and choose frugality as a way of life.

- Increase your income over the years so you can save and expend more.

- Remember: the dollar that goes away does not return.

- Remember that your salary grows every year by 2% to 3% but your saving investment grows by 7% in a compounded form. The more you put into savings the faster you can achieve your capital accumulation goals to retire with financial security.

KNOW YOUR EXPENSES WELL

Necessary expenses are those that are required to meet the basic needs of an individual or family and cannot be dispensed with. Examples include basic expenses for food, electricity, water and sewage, heating, telephone, internet and television, clothes for work and for the children in school, school expenses, gasoline and maintenance of a car, repairs and maintenance of the house, etc.

Discretionary expenses are those that are not serving a basic need but rather are serving a desire to have or consume something extra. These include special products and services that we learn about through skillful advertising and marketing techniques of commercial entities (half- price liquidations, additional discounts if a credit card is opened, etc.). Many times, we buy things similar or identical to what we already have: clothes, tools, articles for the kitchen, shoes etc.

There is another type of expense besides discretionary expense (consumption) and investment expenditure. The following is important to remember:

- House payments (rental, mortgage) are necessary because we must have a roof over our heads.

- For many, the payment of a mortgage is also an investment because it accumulates capital as we pay the loan. In addition, the house accumulates value over time. At the end of 30 years, once the mortgage is paid, we have substantial capital.

- We must not forget that owning a house also has expenses: maintenance, repairs, insurance, interest, payment of real estate taxes, replacing or repairing kitchen equipment, heating, air conditioning and other mechanical elements of a house. These expenses could fall into the category of necessary and capital expenses because they increase the value of the house.

- If we do not have a mortgage, we must pay rent. This can be considered a consumption expense because at the end of the month we do not accumulate any value in our name. It is "lost" money as is utilities. However, renting has several advantages, e.g., no real estate taxes, insurances and other expenses to maintain the house or apartment.

- The loan on a car, truck, or other transportation vehicle is also a necessary expense that we must incur every month to be able to get to work. Some people consider this a consumption expense: at the end of the payment period there remains a very diminished residual value. The alternatives at that time include to continue using the vehicle until its value virtually disappears (and may be donated to an NGO) or use the residual value to buy another vehicle.

To control your expenses, try to buy fewer things and pay less for what you buy. Many times, the quality of the cheapest is like the quality of the more expensive. The difference is often created by the marketing of the product and not because there is a noticeable difference between the products.

Even if there is a quality difference, it is not necessary to always choose the most expensive item. For example, we can buy a house or apartment in a luxury neighborhood or in a neighborhood that better reflects our income, choose a Toyota Corolla or a more expensive Lexus; buy high fashion or more common brand clothes, or eat at a luxury restaurant or a regular one, etc.

Many times, a person may make a fool of him-herself by consuming products and services of high price, when these clearly do not correspond to his/her actual income. The behavior is seen as extravagant, mostly made to impress those around them. But it comes at a high economic cost.

The way we spend our income on goods and services determines if we can one day be economically independent or will continue for a longer period paying debts, living in fantasy and ending up retiring with financial insecurity.

THE PSYCHOLOGICAL FACTOR IN SHOPPING.

For some individuals it is very difficult to control expenses. There are several reasons that explain this attitude. A very important influence is the way one was educated by his/her parents. We know that children are constantly observing us and tend to imitate what we do. If we spend without control, if they see us buying impulsively, if we load everything on the credit cards without thinking about the financial consequences, then the children will understand that it is permissible for them to do the same.

Much of the spending culture is psychological in nature. Many of our purchases are driven by impulse, tricks of our imagination that show fantastic images of what we would do with the items we buy, plus other pressures that push us to buy immediately without thinking,

This psychological factor is exploited by marketing companies which use advertising techniques that are almost irresistible to an average person. The permanent extensive and sophisticated advertising on products through TV, radio, magazines, newspapers, internet, blogs, movies, road signs and vehicles is always with us.

The presentation of merchandise in stores is tailored to human impulses. The stores display the merchandise in strategic places and in a way that the casual customer is tempted to buy, either for the sale price, a gift rebate, or opening a credit card that brings additional discounts.

The more you spend, the more you get used to the pleasure of bringing new things home. Things that were bought, thinking about decorating the house or for use in the kitchen, the bathrooms, the garage, for maintenance of the house, the garden, or the car. Also, we buy clothes, shoes and jewelry with which we imagine we will improve our appearance and impress those around us. Such things most likely are not necessary, but rather only short-term cravings.

To begin to feel the over-consumption spread throughout our society just go to garage and moving sales to realize the number of things that accumulate unnecessarily, things that we barely use. Many of these things are still new, in their original packaging. It is a matter of opening our closets, examining our garages, opening the kitchen cabinets to get a better sense of what we have accumulated almost without thinking.

Alternately, many times the things we accumulate, but don't use, deteriorate and, in the end, be must thrown away. This is the case for food, cleaning chemicals, some tools and clothing. What a financial loss when we buy them with credit cards paying high interest rates that may, at least, double their price in the long term.

For many people, shopping and buying things is a form of recreation. Walking through shopping centers and supermarkets motivates us to buy. When we enter a clothes shop and start looking, touching and imagining, we become enticed with offers at apparently very attractive prices.

For others shopping is a way to combat frustrations or appease sadness or depression. Buying something that we like gives us pleasure, allows us to forget about our hardships for a while. Rich people often do it without consequence. But middle and lower-income people suffer. And they have regrets later when the bills come. This exacerbates their frustrations and emotional problems.

FINANCIAL FACTORS OF EXPENDING

Financial factors refer to the magnitude of the expense and the form of payment. If we had to pay with cash, we could immediately see the economic sacrifice we are making when buying something. We realize immediately that our money is going for good.

When we pay using a credit card, we do not feel that immediate impact. As noted above, commercial advertising on quality, quantity, prices, rebates or liquidations can be misleading. We realize the amount of money we are going to spend only when facing the cashier. We still pass the credit card and pay without discussion or second thoughts.

The same happens when we buy through the internet: paying with a credit card on the internet does not have an impact like when we pay cash.

Regrets come later when we see the detailed credit card statement at the end of the month. Some credit card holders return things a few days later, but stores are becoming more reluctant to accept items on return because of abuses that may have been committed, e.g., partially used items, returns coming only many months after purchases. An additional problem is that many people do not review their credit card statements in detail. They only look at the minimum balance they must pay, missing the opportunity to assess how they are spending their income.

Even more, we know that the credit card allows us to pay only a small amount each month, approximately 1% of the balance we owe. This may be enough to "justify" the expense because it does not seem to affect much our cash availability at the end of the month. However, when we have several cards and we are saturating all of them, the balances owed slowly increase almost without us realizing it.

This is a deception that we create for ourselves because we are motivated by an uncontrolled desire to buy something without looking at the full financial consequences. What we do not think about is that the accumulated balance owed will be paid at a high interest rate.

Depending on one's credit report, that interest can reach almost 30% which means paying more than double the original price.

The argument of businesses is that commercial companies seek to make immediately available to consumers the widest variety of products and services at the lowest possible prices. To do that they offer credit that can be paid with very low monthly payments over a long period of time. The idea is that everyone wins: consumers with low prices and with the possibility of immediately having the products they want, companies with higher profits and the government with higher income from sales taxes.

The above is true up to a certain point, mainly when the consumer buys products or services that they now really need and that are not merely just a whim or impulse purchase in response to exceptional advertising of the company involved. In the end neither the so-called low prices nor the payment plans are always beneficial for the consumer.

Sales techniques are nowadays very advanced, and are based on economic, psychological, cultural, ethnic, racial, age, and local studies. It is very difficult for an individual to overcome these enticements.

In the 21st century it is now possible to analyze gigantic amounts of information through increasingly sophisticated super computers and software. Every day commercial institutions study information about purchases that they collect from consumers. This information is in invoices, sales tickets, credit cards, bank accounts, etc. These data sources are gold mines from which valuable information can be extracted to improve corporate decisions about production, distribution, financing and sale of their products.

Financial institutions and banks that grant credit cards can examine the details of purchases that people have made in a day or month. Supermarkets examine in detail, product by product, what was sold in a day. They can do it by the hour, minutes, seconds.

This is very important because they must restock, calculate profits by product, examine what is sold or not sold, and changes in the tastes of people. As supermarkets are in neighborhoods with well-defined characteristics, they can select products for that clientele and tailor prices, liquidations, commercial propaganda and other selling tools.

The same goes for the big department stores that sell all kinds of products and the mega companies that supply them, the latter also directly flooding society with commercial propaganda.

Commercial companies are improving their sales techniques and commercial propaganda aided by technology that advances dramatically every year. Not only has the "shopping experience" improved in malls where they offer all kinds of services, presentations, entertainment, products in lighted stores and beautiful sales designs, but also through the internet in online "shopping" systems. Customers are easier to access all over the world.

It is easy to conclude that for the consumer it is almost impossible to overcome the temptations being put forth by commercial and financial companies. But an educated consumer aware of their financial situation can control this situation.

The sad thing is that many of us are working to pay credit card interest (and penalties that may be added for late payments) which only goes to the profits of issuing banks and other financial institutions. At the same time, we lose the opportunity to create healthier retirement funds. *We could end up working all our productive life to pay interest, penalties and commissions on our credit cards without even being fully aware of it.*

It is very difficult to give a fool-proof formula to control expenses. That depends on you and your spending habits, culture and discipline. To do this you must be honest with yourself and make realistic analyses of *why* you spend your income for which you work so hard, continuing to do this throughout your life.

WHAT CAN WE DO?

We must learn to live with less. The key word is frugality.

IMPORTANT: frugality does not mean living miserably. It is about consuming in an intelligent way, buying what is necessary in quality and quantity, avoiding waste, unnecessary consumption and accumulation of expensive things.

We must learn to live at a level of consumption a little below what would correspond to our income. This is one of the most valuable secrets of those who are now millionaires.

What we consume or use reflects our level of maturity, personal discipline, common sense and good judgment. It is our projection to the world that surrounds us: home, car, clothes, food, ornaments, accessories.

Remember that we are not better in the eyes of society because we consume more and more expensive things. A frugal and disciplined person gives a better impression overtime than one who spends without control.

This means we should consume according with our income and our saving and investment goals to achieve economic independence.

Do not forget that almost everything we consume will have alternative choices in terms of quality and quantity. We can buy something generic (clothing, food, medicine) or the higher-price brands. The difference in quality is usually not very large and more standard quality can normally satisfy the needs of an average person. In the supermarket we can buy preserves of the supermarket brand or a famous corporation. The same approach can be used for clothes and most of the products and services we need in our daily lives.

REMEMBER: EVERY DOLLAR THAT GOES OUT DOES NOT COME BACK

Above all we must develop and cultivate a practical, disciplined approach to spending that ensures we are realistic when we decide what to buy. If the purchase is necessary, is it possible to postpone or is it something we want but do not need. To check the "need", we can imagine whether after one or two uses we will forget about that product and it will become part of what we accumulate. Other possibilities include to obtain a generic or second-hand product or decide that something we already have at home can adequately replace the desired item.

Do not forget to visit websites dedicated to helping the consumer practice frugality. You will find many ideas about how to be more informed, conservative and economical consumers not only in how to select purchases but also how to finance them.

Finally, do not forget that liquidation prices are deceptive. The original high price probably was for those who do not mind spending or getting into debt. It is common that those liquidation prices recover the store cost for the specific item. They may lower prices slowly to gain additional profits. The store may mark a price as original and then reduce it by 50%. It is a policy to make believe it is a bargain.

In other words, we must be careful to understand what we are seeing. Sometimes we compare prices between products, but the products are different. The one we are now seeing at the store may be of less value than the one we have in mind or we may have seen at another store, but we cannot be sure. This is a common predicament specially with electronics where there are too many models and versions which are very difficult to compare.

It is possible that the one for sale is of lower quality than another model, but both are so similar that you cannot tell the difference. You may end up buying a lower quality product for more.

SPENDING STRATEGY- BOTTOM LINE

Plan well before going shopping. It is always useful to sit down at the dining room table to make a shopping list with one's spouse or friend or partner and with the children and be very realistic and practical about what you want to buy and could pay. This includes analyzing alternatives prices, qualities, quantities, models, type of stores, liquidations, coupons and real needs. You must make this planning session a routine thing. Avoid shopping without planning and analyzing what to buy. Be aware of how you spend your money.

Avoid going for a walk simply wandering around shops and supermarkets. They are full of temptations designed by professionals to make you buy.

Become a role model for teaching your children. They learn by observing. Explain to them why you are buying something, what are the advantages or disadvantages of that purchase over alternatives. This will also help you to assess and verbalize the reason for the purchase.

Avoid creating illusions or fantasies as justification for using or consuming things. These are the tricks that our unconscious plays on us that are motivated by commercial propaganda. Learn to defend yourself against advertising and defend your dollars.

Avoid compulsive purchases, those we do without thinking. To defend yourself, put your mind in blank and move to another place when you are confronted by the desire to buy something. Just buy what you have on your list, the one you have prepared in advance, especially if you made the list with your spouse, partner or children.

Visualize your finances all the time. How much have you accumulated in your retirement fund, how far are you from reaching your savings goal, how much do you owe on your credit card, mortgage, cars. This will help you to be more frugal and evaluate the importance of careful spending.

Again, make a shopping list with alternative and cheaper generic products. Remember that we are not more for what we consume but for our ability to live reasonably well.

Postpone the decision to buy. Make a mental effort and wait until tomorrow to buy something. Eliminate the urgent nature of purchases. Nothing is urgent. Everything can wait, if we want. Waiting gives us time to think better and do more research about what we want to buy. Maybe we do not need it after all. It's good to be evaluating all the time if what we want to buy is worth it.

This brings us to what economists call opportunity cost. What is the alternative use of the money that we are going to spend? Is the purchase superfluous or necessary? This is a good mental exercise. For example, if we do not buy that tool we think is very necessary for some household work or that item for the kitchen, the money that we "save" can be used to pay a larger amount of the minimum on our credit card. We lose that "opportunity" to pay an existing debt when we buy that tool or kitchen item instead.

An alternative to not buying is to change the item for something less expensive and in smaller quantity. This is very possible to do in a supermarket where there are multiple possibilities at different prices.

The amount we buy is important because many times we find ourselves throwing away the surplus, for example, of food because it is spoiled or other food staples that accumulate in the kitchen cupboard or refrigerator.

And again, as a reminder about an important shopping strategy, there are products that can be bought second hand and satisfy your taste just as much or better than new ones. I'm thinking of furniture, appliances, carpets, paintings, ornaments, porcelain, jewelry, and accessories in general. The feeling when buying intelligently reinforces the idea of being frugal especially when you have debts or a mortgage.

Get used to analyzing the financial statements of your credit cards, mortgage and car. This will help you visualize the opportunity cost of not having that income. Remember what you do not spend you can use to pay debts or make a deposit in your savings or pension account.

The saddest thing, the mother of a lady friend of ours told me, is to get old and sick and also be poor. This lady and her husband had had a good income throughout their lives, but the majority was wasted. Unfortunately, the husband liked to pretend to have what he did not have. "It's a good sign to show that my business is going well," he said. My husband was a very intelligent and social man, this lady told us, full of friends, but also of debts. By dying he left me alone with few savings. Now I live on social security income and help from my children.

THE SAVINGS STRATEGY

Saving represents sacrifices because it forces us not to buy things today in order to save for investing to achieve our goals of financial independence and economic security. These goals are discussed in detail in other chapters and listed here again.

- Retire with a Social Security pension and Medicare benefits.
- Retire with a pension fund (s) that yields at least 80% of your expenses before retirement.
- Create a personal savings fund for emergencies and other needs.
- Do not have debts at the time of retirement.
- Have a house paid and clean of obligations.
- Arrive at the time of retirement with good health and energy.

This chapter discuss some underlining principles and questions each person, or couple will want to consider as part of their saving strategy.

SAVE FOR YOU FIRST

There are many articles on topics of family finances that recommend, first, making a family budget. This would allow you to set spending limits in each category and define the amount you can save. If you do this in a digital worksheet like Excel, you can simulate different spending alternatives until you find one that most closely matches your needs and personal approach to consumption and savings.

Second, to effectively control your expenses, some articles also suggest that you make a list of all the expenses you have each day, even the smallest ones that may be only a few cents. If you do it every day, if possible, in a notebook (expenses journal) you will become more aware of how you spend your money and areas where you might change your spending habit to be more frugal and thriftier.

This is a rational way to proceed for disciplined people with a firm commitment to save, accumulate income and build capital. I have met people manage their finances in that way. However, this is not the common situation. My experience tells me that this way of generating savings is rarely practiced by most people.

Many start by making a budget and keeping a diary of expenses, but daily life competes for your time, especially if you have a family with children and both spouses work. Daily demands of living, going to the supermarket, laundry, cleaning the house, caring for the garden, car, maintenance of the house overwhelm best intentions. These basic chores take all the hours of the day and make it difficult to keep detailed records of expenses.

Monitoring all daily expenses requires time and discipline. Imagine writing down all the expenses that you make in a day in a notebook or in slips of paper to pass at the end of the day to the notebook and then at the end of the month to transfer this to your worksheet for comparison with your budget for that month.

I discovered many years ago that the most practical way to save is the one that is AUTOMATIC. I remember when I started working in a bank, fresh out of high school, the check that I received at the end of the month was the money that I could spend in full. Why? Because that check was for an amount that was my available salary after my employer deducted my social security taxes, income taxes, contributions to my retirement fund and health insurance.

I never had problems with this system and my life automatically adjusted to the income level that the monthly check allowed. That was what I received and that was what I spent. In this way, the custom of securing my retirement fund was created in me automatically, partly because the bank demanded it, but later out of conviction.

The important thing was the AUTOMATIC deduction of my contribution to the pension fund out of my monthly salary. I did not have to make any special effort during the month. The deduction guaranteed that I made monthly savings. I knew that I was contributing to my retirement and my health, but in an almost unconscious way because it seemed that it was obligatory to do so. Nobody doubted the need for these deductions because in the end they were for the benefit of oneself. It was the most logical thing to do. We all thought that way.

Eventually I asked the accounting office to deduct an extra sum every month because I planned to take a vacation and knew it would be easier for me to have that extra amount saved automatically. I was very young, and temptations to spend frivolously were very great.

In the end I did not take that vacation because circumstances changed, but I kept saving that extra money anyway. It made me feel good to have a little bit of extra capital.

I was beginning to be more financially secure, more disciplined, more responsible with my money as a young adult. This was a beginning of my saving habits. Almost instinctively I kept this account quiet, in a way it was my secret.

That experience led me to conclude that saving depends in large part on our mental attitude toward spending. For most of us it is a permanent struggle between the impulse to buy and borrow versus to save some of what we earn to meet unforeseen needs and plan for the future.

In the end it is about saving first and consuming what is left.

HOW MUCH WILL OUR EXPENSES BE WHEN WE RETIRE?

That is one of the most common questions that many individuals and couples ask, especially when they reach middle age (40 to 50 years old). The question is, will we have enough income at retirement (65 years old) to live comfortably for the rest of our days? Others who may be more ambitious wonder if they could retire before that age for example at 59 ½ years when one can start taking monthly payments without paying fines.

Experience has shown that a couple achieves economic independence when they obtain a monthly income adjusted for inflation, from their various retirement and saving funds and social security, that will cover at least 80% of the average expenses in the last three years before retiring.

There are several theories about how to estimate future expenses. Some authors suggest that 80% of pre-retirement expenses is a reasonable percentage because several expenses go away with retirement. These include payment of labor tax, contributions to an emergency fund, contributions to a pension fund, ideally the mortgage is paid and the couple or individual is free of all other mayor debts.

For their part, the children ideally are already making their living independently so that expenses for their studies and maintenance are gone. Finally, the couple, now alone, may choose to move to a smaller house and even another area where prices are lower. With all these changes some believe they could live in retirement with a lower percentage of pre-retirement expenses, e.g. around 70% or less.

Other advisers think it is better to calculate a higher percentage of pre-retirement expenses (90%). The rationale here is that after retirement there may be new expenses such as medical and dental care, pharmacy expenses, more vacation trips inside and outside the country, more frequent meals out of the house with friends and family, and more entertainment such as the cinema, theater, concerts. Many times, also, retirees must continue to help their children or grandchildren financially, including with college expenses.

It is difficult to offer a general rule, but usually the retired person or couple needs a few years to establish a level of spending adjusted to match their new needs and new income. Undoubtedly spending levels also depend on the spending habits of each couple, their social status, health condition, family situations and other factors.

My recommendation is that as soon as possible one must learn to live with less than what one receives as income and without getting into new debt. Be as financially prepared as possible for what may come, have good health, enough funds for the home and other basic insurance and emergencies.

HOW MUCH CAPITAL SHOULD WE HAVE ACCUMULATED IN OUR RETIREMENT FUNDS TO BE ABLE TO RETIRE DECENTLY?

Let's look to a scenario using 80%. A person should save enough so that, at retirement, he/she earns an income from investments (social security, retirement fund and investment accounts) to finance at least 80% of the expenses averaged over the last three years of work.

Example: A couple at the time of retirement had an income of $100,000 per year but spent on average only $80,000. The way to finance these expenses post-retirement could be as follows:

Social security income	$37,200
Income from your pension funds	$42,800

The question now is how much capital the couple needs in its pension funds to generate $42,300 a year. The answer to this question is that the couple at retirement should need an accumulated capital of approximately $845,000. This sum is expressed in today's dollars and assumes an investment return rate of 5% after discounting for inflation.

SOME IDEAS ON HOW BUID-UP YOUR PENSION FUND

The other question is how we can accumulate that capital, how much should we save each month in our pension funds during the entire period of our working life, estimated at 40 years.

The first rule, the GOLDEN RULE, is the one mentioned earlier.

- Save first and consume later.

- Save in the form of automatic deductions from of your gross salary every month.

When you are young (25-35 years) your income is relatively low, and you are making every effort to obtain income with maximum benefits. In the first years of a marriage there are many expenses. You will need things to make a home and perhaps even put together the down payment to buy a house. In these circumstances, it is likely there will be little extra for your pension fund given obligations associated with creating an emergency fund, paying social security and health insurance and mortgage. In any case, the ideal would be for the couple to save at least 5-10% of their income per year for their pension funds.

Following this scenario, by about age 35, a couple should have saved in their pension funds the equivalent of 160% of the gross income they receive annually at that point. If at 35-40 years of age a couple has an income, for example, of $65,000, the pension fund should be $107,250.

As one gets to the 35/45 age range, income normally increases. It is a period of professional and employee growth. There is more experience and confidence in what one does. There are more responsibilities, potential promotions and increases in salaries and benefits. As the latter increase, additional savings can be made to pension funds ideally reaching 15% or more of total annual gross income. This strategy balances-out the lowest savings made in the previous decade.

Continuing with the same scenario, by about age 45, a couple should have saved in the pension funds the equivalent of 300% of the gross income they receive annually at that time. If at 45-55 years of age a couple receives income of $80,000, they should have in their pension funds, the sum of $240,000.

The decade of 45/55 marks the intellectual, professional and labor peak of a worker, whatever their specialty: qualified employee, technician, professional, manager, small entrepreneur. The fruits of training, university studies, experience and work productivity are rewarded with greater responsibilities and commonly higher income and benefits.

At the same time family expenses should begin to decrease, the house mortgage is paid or almost paid, the children are leaving for university, mayor debts are reduced. At this point, savings into pension funds should increase to 20-25%. Assuming a couple by age 55 is receiving $90,000 of combined income, their retirement fund should have grown to 600% of what they receive annually, in this case $540,000.

At 55/65 years of age the financial situation of the couple should generally progress along the lines of the previous decade. Savings should be able to increase even more. By age 65 a couple should have saved in their retirement funds the equivalent of 800% of what they receive annually. At this point it is very possible that this couple is receiving a combine income of $110,000 which means that by about age 65 they should have accumulated in their retirement funds the sum of $880,000

Remember these figures represent the pension funds of a couple, i.e. two people who have worked for 40 years and have saved an average of 15% of their annual gross income during that time. These are approximate figures that can help to give an idea of what could be achieved with the discipline of saving and intelligent investing of those savings through retirement funds.

Do not get discouraged if you have not managed to reach the recommended sum by 45 years of age. It is possible to recover from previous periods of less savings up to a point. In the last 20 years of working life savings can be substantially increased to ensure a retirement fund that allows you to live decently in retirement. But that requires discipline. The sooner you start catching up, the more likely you will be achieving your retirement goals.

Finally, the story does not end here. A couple needs to have accumulated $946,000 invested for at least 30 years at 5% rate of return after discounting inflation to generate the $47,300 per year mentioned above. This amount added to the annual income of social security (estimated at $29,700) and to income from your emergency savings account ($3,000) gives a total of $80,000 per year, the sum that this couple will need under this scenario to cover its expenses.

THE INVESTMENT STRATEGY

One of the most important features of an investment strategy is simplicity. This allows us to understand what we are doing, and facilitates conversations with financial institutions such as Fidelity, Schwab, Vanguard and other similar financial corporations.

Within pension funds and other investment accounts where you have your savings, you can buy and sell stocks, bonds, CDs, mutual funds and other types of financial instruments. This can be done directly from your computer by entering your account with an entry password or through a financial agent at the institution where you have that account. In this latter case, you must pay for their services.

IMPORTANT. Keep in mind that in the last 15 years workers received income from salaries and wages that increased at a rate of about 2.5 % a year. For their part, the investors have been receiving income from interest, dividends, and capital gains at an annual rate of return of about 10% a year. No question the latter is the most effective mechanism to create wealth, income and opportunities and it is for all available only if you know how to use it.

In this chapter we assume that the couple has two incomes that together amount to between $50,000 and $100,000 per year. These incomes are considered in economic terms as low and medium incomes respectively for a family of four: two parents and two children. In this chapter we consider the following family income categories:

FAMILY INCOME CATEGORIES	FROM	TO
POVERTY	0	24,500
LOW INCOME	24,501	49,000
LOW MIDDLE INCOME	49.001	75,000
MIDDLE INCOME	75,000	100,000
MIDDLE HIGH INCOME	100,001	150,000
HIGH INCOME	150,001	250,000

Even though you may be currently participating in a pension fund and making investments in them it is advisable to make an assessment each year about where you are at that time in relation to your finances and investments. There are always possibilities to improve your investment strategy and to become more aware of new options.

Even at the risk of repeating some investment concepts I think it is important to review them again here.

BASIC CONCEPTS

What is a stock?

A stock is a document that shows you own a part of the capital of a company. The capital of a company consists of all the shares (stock) that it sold to form that capital. The shares of a company have the value that the buyers give them in the Stock Exchange. This value depends on the ability of the company to generate profits, which are periodically distributed to the owners of the shares in the form of dividends. Therefore, a shareholder benefits from the dividends he/her receives and the increase (or decrease) in value that his/her shares can have in the stock market.

What is a bond?

Bonds represent a loan that a company or a government institution assumes for a defined period of time at a given interest rate. The bond document indicates the name of the seller, its value in dollars, the interest rate it pays and for how long. Bonds are sold to the public through financial institutions or the stock exchange.

For example: A company needs money to make an investment. It could sell a bond with the following characteristics: price $1,000; period to maturity 10 years; interest rate 7% per year. The buyer/owner of the bond receives the interest from the bond every 6 months and at the end of ten years receives the original $1,000 back. The owner of this bond can sell it in the stock market to recover its capital at any time before maturity but at the price offered by the market at that time. This is the value of the bond in the so-called secondary market.

Continuing this example, the two most important elements to consider in a bond in the secondary market are price and interest rate. The market price depends on the existing interest rate in the market (higher or lower than the bond's initial rate), the time left for the bond to reach its tenth anniversary and the quality of the company that issues it. In this case, if the interest rate in the market is less than the original 7%, the bond will have a higher price than the original $1,000 to compensate for the lower interest rate. If the rate is greater than 7% the bond price will be lower. But again, whoever is the owner at the time of expiration will receive the $1,000, that is, the original price.

What is a Certificate of Deposit?

The Certificate of Deposit (CD) is a financial instrument used to invest money in the short term. Commercial banks and other financial institutions sell CDs. These certificates can usually be of any amount, but it is common that they are of fixed amounts like $1,000, $5,000, $10,000, $15,000 $25,000, $100,000. These are purchased for a fixed period: 60 days, 3 months, 6 months, one year, etc. You are paid an amount set at an annual percentage of interest. If you withdraw the money before its time of maturity you pay a fine. CDs are insured by the government up to the amount of $50,000.

In recent years the interest rate of 1-year CDs has been below 1%. You can buy them directly at a bank where they will give you a certificate where the details of this deposit are indicated: its amount, time period, interest rate, penalties. There is a lot of experience and information about this type of investment. You can find it online.

What are Mutual Funds?

Mutual funds are financial entities that invest funds or savings from individual investors, corporations, pension funds and other organizations. These entities have a board of directors, managers, administrators and financial specialists.

The funds they receive are invested in shares from a list of corporations the fund managers and their board of directors have chosen. These corporations are chosen according to their capacity to generate profits continuously, be well managed, have an attractive price in the capital market (Stock Exchange) and pay dividends. A relatively small part of a total mutual fund can be invested in bonds and money instruments.

The total value of the shares, bonds, money reserves and other investments that the mutual fund has purchased is divided by a specific number of units. These units are called mutual fund shares. In other words, the value of an action of a mutual fund is equal to the total value of all the investments of the fund divided by the number of units of that mutual fund. The shares of the fund should not be confused with the shares of the corporations that the fund purchases with the savings.

The net profits of the mutual fund (dividends and capital gains less expenses of the fund) are distributed among the shares held by each individual or entity.

PURCHASE OF SHARES AND INDIVIDUAL BONDS

Think twice before buying stock (shares) of specific corporations. There are very few individual investors who have enough knowledge, interest and experience to decide what shares of corporations to buy. The financial information available to evaluate the economic situation of the corporations is extensive, of good quality, but complex. It requires specialized knowledge in finance to invest directly in corporate shares.

The alternative is to do it through specialists from financial institutions. But this alternative is expensive: you must pay fees, commissions, administrative expenses, sales taxes and other costs. The same is true with respect to government or corporate bonds. These expenses are incurred every time you buy or sell.

It is true that you can open an account in the U.S. Treasury and directly buy government bonds, but this also requires knowledge and monitoring as an individual.

Even more difficult is having the discipline to follow up periodically on the stocks and bonds that you have purchased directly or through a specialist. The longer the list of stocks of individual corporations and bonds that you buy the more complicated is this task. Not to mention the emotional effect on the investor of the highs and lows of the stock market in relation to each type of share that is held.

Studies have shown that many individual investors sell their shares in panic when the stock market falls and buy optimistically when the stock market has risen. A classic formula for losing capital.

ADVANTAGES OF MUTUAL FUNDS
THE IMPORTANCE OF DIVERSITY IN INVESTMENTS

Mutual funds were created with the objective of reducing the risk of investing in individual corporations. As the mutual fund buys shares of hundreds of companies, the values of some of them fall and others rise so that over time it is expected that more will rise in value than those that fall.

In case there is a crisis and stock market values fall, there will always be some corporations whose shares rise in price so that the decline will be more moderate. If you buy shares of a single company, for example, General Motors, your total risk depends on the economic results of a single company. If you buy shares of a mutual fund your risk is distributed in among the hundreds of companies that you buy through the fund.

Mutual funds offer a large diversity of instruments for investing. They protect investors from high risk, transfer most of the decisions and their administration to qualified analysts of the financial institutions. In the medium and long term they generally obtain better returns than can be obtained by owning shares of corporations individually and it is an easy mechanism through which to make investments. In addition, it is easy to obtain information about the returns, costs, prices, and levels of risk of the different mutual funds that exist in the market which facilitates comparison for decision making.

THE IMPORTANCE OF CONSIDERING YOUR TOLERANCE FOR RISK

Risk is the probability that exists in the Stock Exchange that the stocks and bonds that you bought lose value due to a crisis or mismanagement of a company.

Each individual or family has a certain risk tolerance that is important to consider when starting or restarting an investment process. This tolerance depends mainly on the age of the saver. It is obvious that the younger savers have more tolerance because they have a longer life in front of them to recover financially if the shares fall in value. They will probably choose mutual stock and bond funds that guarantee at the least an average annual return of 7% in the long term.

In contrast, those who are close to retirement will likely prefer to invest their savings in low risk instruments such as government bonds, which are the safest instruments that exist in the market. Their long-term rates of return currently fluctuate around 3%.

Those between 25 and 65 years of age have all the risk options available to them and many choose investment types that have an average risk, such as investing 60% of their savings in mutual funds of corporate stock and 40% in government bonds and high-quality corporations. The following table shows some recommended portfolio options for couples who have an average risk tolerance:

PORTFOLIO TYPES PER AGE	PORTFOLIO PROPORTION
25 - 35 YEARS	90% STOCK 10% CASH
35 - 45	80 STOCK/ 10 BONDS/ 10 CASH
45 - 55	70/20/10
55 - 65	60/30/10
65 - 75	50/40/10
75 - 85	20/70/10
85 -	90/10

Today no one puts his/her savings "under the mattress." However, there are people of all ages who have very low tolerance for risk of losing their savings. So, they keep their savings in a bank checking account or bank savings account, even though the interest paid is almost nothing. If you discount the inflation from the interest you receive from such a bank account, you will be losing money or purchasing power.

An important factor to consider is the loss of the purchase value of your savings due to inflation. This is a risk that sometimes goes unnoticed. If your pension fund at the end of the year yields 7% and inflation is 2%, your return is 5%.

Therefore, it is important that you think carefully about your risk tolerance and select an appropriate mix of investment instruments that respond to your risk level while at the same time obtaining the needed rate of return in the long term.

THE IMPORTANCE OF THE LONG TERM

Mutual funds are an ideal means to make investments in pension funds. It was never intended that these funds were to buy and sell shares or other financial instruments in the short term. The long-term time frame guarantees receiving the benefits of compounded interest, deferred taxes and monthly automatic savings.

The long-term view also helps one psychologically to overcome the ups and downs of the stock market from economic cycles. The potential of long-term investing is an accumulation of a significant capital at the end of 30 or 40 years.

THE IMPORTANCE OF BEGINNING TO MAKE CONTRIBUTIONS TO A PENSION FUND AT AN EARLY AGE

The later you start contributing savings to a pension fund, the lower will be your capital accumulation and the lower will be your income when you retire. Ideally, you should start contributing at age 25 and do so in an uninterrupted manner until age 65 (before or after) depending on when you decide to retire.

There is always the opportunity to catch up with bigger contributions when you are older, have higher income and lower expenses. But that requires more discipline and as much time as possible before you retire. The key to achieving good results is the length of time you keep your investments in the stock market. If you start late to make contributions the only way to catch up will be to make larger contributions to your pension funds and other investment accounts in later years.

THE IMPORTANCE OF COMPOUNDED GROWTH OVER A LONG PERIOD OF TIME[7]

Investments should be allowed to accumulate interest and dividends for the longest period possible to benefit from the compounded effect as explained below.

- Dividends and interest from the investment of your contributions to pension funds are added every month to the capital that you accumulate.

- Example: at the end of the first year, let's say, a couple (two incomes) made a total contribution equivalent to 10% of their gross income. If their income totaled $60,000, the 10%

7. If you receive a lump sum ($50,000) when you are relatively young (25 to 30 years old) and deposit it in SP500 for 30 years with a nominal return of 7% it would growth to $380,613

that they saved and invested in their retirement funds would be $6,000. That sum if invested in mutual funds, at the end of that year would have an increase of 7% (historical average) from dividends, and interest. This means the value of the shares $6,000 plus 7% of $6000 ($ 420) or $6420.

- In the second year their retirement fund starts on January 1st with $6,420. This sum will grow again by 7% but over the $6,420 which will give in return $449. In total at the end of this second year the balance of the account will be $6,420 plus $ 49 or $6,869.

- This means that the growth rate of your investments (7%) is calculated on your contributions plus the accumulated earnings of previous years.

- NOW, pay attention: as you continue to contribute 10% of your income each year, the growth of your capital in your retirement funds accelerates enormously. In year 2 you have already accumulated the capital of year one which is $6,420 to which you add the contribution of year two ($6,000), which gives you a total of $ 12,420. But this figure grows by 7% (historical growth) which gives a total of $13,289.

- As you can see in the Tables below, the increase of your pension fund grows substantially with the calculation of 7% compounded on your annual contributions to your pension funds plus what has been accumulating in previous years.

- THE MOST IMPORTANT THING TO UNDERSTAND: A couple saving $500 monthly ($250 each) in their pension funds in 30 years using the 7% example will accumulate the sum of $612,438 and in 40 years the sum of $1,287,657.

This table shows that a small change in the rate of return of 1% (from 6% to 7%) translates into a big change in a period of 30 or

40 years. At the same time, a change in the term of the investment from 30 years to 40 years also generates large changes in the returns, whether these are 6% or 7%.

COMPOUNDED INCREASE OF AN ANNUAL INVESTMENT OF $6,000 MADE ONLY ONCE.								
	YEAR 1	YEAR 2	YEAR 3	YEAR 4	YEAR 5	YEAR 15	YEAR 30	YEAR 40
Inicial contribution	6,000							
Carry over from previous year	0	6420	6,869	7,350	7,865			
ANNUAL RETURN AT 7%	420	449	481	515	551			
TOTAL ACCUMULATED CAPITAL	6,420	6,869	7,350	7,865	8,415	16554	47,674	89,847
Annual returns include interest, dividends and capital gains reinvested.								

COMPOUNDED INCREASE OF AN ANNUAL INVESTMENT OF $6,000 MADE EVERY YEAR.								
	YEAR 1	YEAR 2	YEAR 3	YEAR 4	YEAR 5	YEAR 15	YEAR 30	YEAR 40
Carry-over prevous year		6,420	13,289	20,640	28,504			
Annual contribution	6,000	6,000	6,000	6,000	6,000			
SUBTOTAL	6,000	12,420	19,289	26,640	34,504			
ANNUAL RETURN AT 7%	420	869	1,350	1,865	2,415			
TOTAL	6,420	13,289	20,640	28,504	36,920	167,328	612,438	1,287,657
Annual returns include interest, dividends and capital gains reinvested.								

ANNUAL RETURNS OF INVESTED FUNDS					
ANNUAL INCOME	ANNUAL SAVING 10%	RETURNS 6% 30 YEARS	RETURNS 7% 30 YEARS	RETURNS 6% 40 YEARS	RETURNS 7% 40 YEARS
$ 50,000	$ 5,000	$ 395,290	$ 472,304	$ 773,810	$ 998,176
$ 60,000	$ 6,000	$ 474,349	$ 566,765	$ 928,572	$ 1,197,811
$ 70,000	$ 7,000	$ 553,407	$ 661,226	$ 1,083,334	$ 1,397,446
$ 80,000	$ 8,000	$ 632,465	$ 755,686	$ 1,238,096	$ 1,597,081
$ 90,000	$ 9,000	$ 711,523	$ 850,147	$ 1,392,858	$ 1,797,716
$ 100,000	$ 10,000	$ 790,582	$ 944,608	$ 1,547,620	$ 1,966,351

THE IMPORTANCE OF DIFFERED TAXES

Dividends, interest and capital gains (if you sell your shares for a higher price than what you paid) require the owner to pay federal income tax every year. If you invest your savings in a pension fund (401k, IRA, ROTH or other similar pension fund) you will not pay taxes on that income until you reach age 59 and a half and decide to withdraw funds from your retirement funds. They are deferred until you reach that age. You can withdraw earlier, but you will pay a fine. You don't need to withdraw funds until you are 70 and half years old when it is mandatory that you start withdrawing funds and paying taxes.

The main idea of this law is that savers of pension funds can use the money equivalent to the taxes they do not pay as part of their capital and benefit from the profits they can get from them. This is a great incentive to save in the pension fund because, as we saw earlier, the long term and compounded growth of investments will substantially increase the accumulation of capital in your pension funds.

THE IMPORTANCE OF AUTOMATICALLY CONTRIBUTING MONTHLY AND THROUGHOUT YOUR WORKING YEARS A MINIMUM OF 10% OF GROSS INCOME.

The most important goal, as we saw above, is to create a flow of savings that generates a compounded accumulation of capital for the longest possible time. The second important goal is to create a minimum monthly savings discipline that is uninterrupted to achieve the objective of capital accumulation. A proven way to do this is through an arrangement with the personnel office where you work to automatically transfer at least 10% monthly to your pension fund.

This automatic way of saving makes it possible to ensure that the savings materialize without your conscious effort. Many workers do not have the inclination or discipline to write a check every month and deposit it in their pension funds. Others are negligent, they just don't do it. Others just forget to make deposits. Then are those who, even before receiving their income, have already spent it.

For their part, employers who have a 401k system have adopted the discipline of making these transfers automatically, leaving the employee the responsibility to request, preferably in writing, that they don't want this automatic deduction anymore. In most cases, employees have accepted this procedure.

If you do not have access to a 401k system, you can ask your company's personnel office to automatically transfer a percentage of your salary to your IRA or ROTH savings account. You can also ask the bank where you have your checking account to transfer a certain amount to your IRA or ROTH account either at that same bank or another financial institution where you have an account.

THE IMPORTANCE OF UNDERSTANDING ECONOMIC CYCLES

Historically, a country's economy has periods of substantial economic growth for a certain number of years until the economy stops growing and its GDP (Gross Domestic Product) begins to fall creating unemployment, reduction of investments, lack of demand and a further reduction of its GDP.

This economic situation is reflected in the values that stocks and bonds have in the stock market, causing a fall in values that are called "corrections" when the stock market drops by 10% or more. In more serious cases when the stock market drops 20% or more (recession), there are national and international alarms and many investors sell their shares in panic when they are at their lowest values.

The important thing for you to remember is that these 10% corrections commonly last for no more than 3 months after which the economy returns to normal and the stock market values begin to rise rapidly. In cases of recession, recovery is 6 months to one year. As an exception, the last recession (2007-2009) lasted almost two years.

Therefore, you MUST NOT panic when the stock market falls and you should not start selling your shares. After a few months you will regret having done that when the stock market begins to rise and exceeds the values you had before the recession or correction. The worst thing you can do is sell when the stock market falls and buy when the stock is at its highest value. But, importantly, you must have your savings in funds of the highest quality in order to benefit from this cycle of ups and downs of the stock market. Later we show you some strategy options.

TYPES OF MUTUAL FUNDS

Active mutual fund. They are called active mutual funds because all financial decisions, their administration and promotion are done by a board and a financial administration, which manages the fund directly, buys and sells shares, monitors, and maintains a group of analysts who study the best options offered by the market. This type of mutual fund is common and there are thousands of them. They are offered by a wide variety of financial institutions and banks.

Mutual funds indexed. To measure the performance of the stock market, independent financial research institutions have been created solely to make lists (indexes) of companies that meet certain characteristics to determine how the prices of the shares on that list behave in the stock market. It's like a virtual mutual fund created just to see what would happen if one bought those shares. The results obtained at the end of a one-year period are compared with the results obtained by the mutual funds actively administered.

There are several indices to compare the performance of active mutual funds. One of the most common is the one created by the Standard & Poor 500 Index (or just the SP500), which contains a list of the 500 corporations in the stock market with high capitalizations, good returns, long duration and excellent administration. Historically, this index has had average results of around 7% per year, which has been better than that obtained by active mutual funds. To obtain the same results, financial institutions have created mutual funds that buy exactly the same shares that are included in that index.

Financial corporations such as Schwab, Fidelity, Vanguard, State Street, Blackrock and others have created index funds related to that index, that is, they buy the same shares that exist in that SP500 list or index. Other indexes are the SP600 (small companies) and the SP400 (medium companies).

For example, Vanguard Corporation has created the Vanguard SP500 index fund; State Street Corporation has created SPDR SP500; Blackrock Corporation has created IShares SP500 IVV 500; Schwab has created Schwab SP500 index; Fidelity has created Fidelity SP500 index. Other financial institutions have also created this type of fund which you can find on the internet.

The shares of these indexed mutual funds can be purchased at most financial institutions and banks, most probably through the one where you have your retirement fund.

An important characteristic of active and indexed mutual funds is that their shares can only be bought and sold at the prices they have at the end of the day: 4 pm on the New York Stock Exchange and Nasdaq Stock Market (an American stock exchange that is the second largest in the world after the New York Stock Exchange).

Mutual funds indexed ETF type. These funds are similar to the indexed mutual funds explained above. The only difference is that fund shares can be bought and sold at any time during the day the stock exchange is open for transactions. That is why they are called "tradable funds in the stock market" or "Exchange Traded Funds" (ETFs). This is an important feature for an investor who wants to buy and sell shares or bonds offered by the market from second to second.

THE IMPORTANCE OF COST IN THE PERFORMANCE OF INVESTMENTS

Trading ordinary mutual funds (active funds) have higher costs than buying stock as an individual. Mutual funds must pay for administration, sales, marketing, promotions, transactions, commissions and the Board that supervises them. In addition, mutual funds buy and sell shares more often following changes in the market to obtain the maximum possible return. Each time they make a transaction, they incur expenses. They have higher turnover of shares.

Indexed mutual funds (passive funds) have lower costs because there are no analysts selecting company stocks: they just buy the shares of the companies listed in the index. In addition, their administration is much simpler and the shares they buy are kept for a longer period, avoiding continuous purchases and sales and the commissions associated with each transaction.

If the active mutual fund declares an 8% return at the end of the year you should deduct its expenses from that return to have the actual rate of return of your pension fund. Ordinary mutual funds can easily reach a cost of 1.5% to 2% per annum, while indexed mutual funds have an annual cost of less than 0.40% and some of them less than 0.10%.

THE IMPORTANCE OF THE ANNUAL PERFORMANCE OF YOUR INVESTMENTS

In practice, there are very few active or ordinary mutual funds capable of overcoming the returns of the indexed mutual funds. Especially since 2017, individual investors and some institutional investors have been transferring their resources to indexed mutual funds. They reach the conclusion that the returns of the latter have been higher than those offered by the funds actively managed by financial institutions, banks and specialized financial companies (e.g. Hedge Funds (investment funds containing a variety of assets, often with complicated portfolios and high risk).

Twice a year the S & P Dow Jones Indices make a study of the returns of index funds and ordinary funds for the last 15 years. The recent studies show that in all categories and types of investment (corporate shares, bonds and money) the performance of indexed funds was higher than that of ordinary mutual funds.

In a table above, I mentioned that a small change in the rate of return on your investments has a great impact on the accumulation of capital in your pension fund. This is an impressive characteristic of the compounding feature of saving and investing.

Several authors have compared investments made in ordinary mutual funds and index funds. Among them, the late John Bogle stands out. He created the financial institution known as Vanguard Investments, one of the largest in the USA, known for its efficiency and honesty in managing the resources of its clients.

Bogle was a pioneer in the 1960s and 1970s in recommending to investors of average income that they should invest in indexed mutual funds, especially those that cover all companies in the stock market, because they have historically higher yields than do active mutual funds. Another investor of great importance, Warren Buffet, has recommended the same.

PORTFOLIOS FOR A PENSION FUND OF A MIDDLE-INCOME INVESTOR (401K, IRA, ROTH-IRA OR OTHER SIMILAR)

Below I lay out my idea of a classic portfolio for an individual investor or a family that has the following characteristics:

- Their ages are between 25 and 55 years
- Save no less than 10% per month of their income and invest it monthly in their pension funds, if possible, automatically.
- Accept an average risk in their investments.
- Accept to invest for the long term until they reach 65 years or more.

Before getting to the portfolio, several general points are worth noting. First, my advice is to invest your savings in an ETF (Exchange Traded Fund). This type of investment allows the individual investor to benefit from all the financial features mentioned above: diversity, long term, compounded accumulation, low costs, deferred taxes, weathering cycles of the stock market, obtaining the average rate of return of the market and, above all, simplicity in management.

Second, in this proposal I advise you to manage and monitor your investments directly from your computer by setting up online access to the 401k, IRA, ROTH, or other similar account that you have (for example, with financial institutions such as Schwab, Fidelity, Vanguard, etc.). This will save you a lot in cost that otherwise would be charged by the institutions managing your investments.

Third, in a 401k account you have a limited number of investment possibilities. These are determined by the employer or the financial institution you hired to manage these accounts. On average, these institutions currently offer 28 types of investments in the form of ordinary, indexed, balanced or target mutual funds.

Fourth, in the case of IRA and ROTH-IRA accounts, they offer more than 10,000 types of mutual funds. You can also buy directly (online) stocks and bonds of corporations, government bonds, certificates of deposit and other investments. Exploring investment opportunities directly from your computer will help you better understand the mechanics of investing, keep you alert about your financial situation and your options, and give you more confidence to manage them.

Fifth, if you cannot do it personally, work through an employee at the financial institution where you have your account. He/she can buy and sell financial instruments for you and give you advice about what to do. This will force you to go periodically to that financial office and get acquainted with those who work there. Try to establish a working relationship with one of them. That employee can teach you how to access your account, make transactions, track and get information about the services offered.

Keep in mind, however, that financial services must be paid for and could become expensive. For example, a financial administrator may require you to pay 1% calculated on the total investments you have in that institution. If you have $300,000 accumulated in your IRA, you could pay $3,000 annually.

In the portfolio example below, I use an 80/20 type formula that is 80% shares (60% shares of US companies, 20% of international companies) and 20% bonds. It is assumed that as you get older, this formula begins to increase the percentage of bonds.

All ETF-indexed mutual funds mentioned below can be purchased through the financial institution where you have your pension fund.

OPTION 1

Consider investing up to 60% of your capital in shares of an ETF fund that includes all the shares traded on the US stock exchange. The great advantage here is that such fund includes shares of large (worth more than $5 billion) medium (worth between $1 billion and $5 billion) and small (worth between $300 million and $2 billion) cap companies in a single indexed fund. Automatically reinvest dividends and continue buying shares every month without fail throughout your working life. Make a religion of this practice. Below, I present three ETF-indexed mutual funds. You might choose only one. For simplicity:

- Vanguard Total Stock Market ETF (VTI)
- Schwab US Broad Market ETF (SCHB)
- IShares Core SP Total US Stock Market ETF (ITOT)

Consider investing up to 20% of your capital in shares of an ETF fund that includes shares of foreign companies from developed and emerging countries. This type of fund is a bit more volatile than the funds of American companies but allows even more diversification (less risk) and convenience. Automatically reinvest dividends and continue buying shares every month. Below, I present three ETF-indexed mutual funds with this feature. You might choose only one, for simplicity:

- Vanguard Total International Stock Index (VGTSX)
- Schwab International Index Fund (SWISX)
- IShares Core MSCI Total International Stock ETF

Consider investing up to 20% of your capital in an ETF fund that includes all the high-quality bonds issued by the US government and corporations. As they usually include large, medium and short-term bonds you can consider this fund as your only investment in bonds. It gives you more diversity, is low cost and has average returns over ordinary bond funds. The following funds are an example of this:

- Vanguard Total Bond Fund
- Schwab Total Bond Market Fund
- I Share Core Total US Bond Market ETF

In summary, with this option you could have a portfolio in your pension fund consisting of only three funds (one from each group mentioned above) that covers practically all investment possibilities. An example would be the following:

- Vanguard Total Stock Market ETF (VTI): 60%

- Schwab International Index Fund (SWISX): 20%

- IShares Core Total US Bond Market ETF (AGG): 20%

OPTION 2

One way to simplify your investments is to put all your monthly savings, automatically, as much as possible, into a single mutual fund that covers the entire spectrum of US stocks such as:

- Vanguard Total Stock Market

- IShares Total Stock Market

- Schwab Total Stock Market Index Fund

These funds include shares of large (SP500), medium (SP400) and small (SP600) corporations that have their shares registered in the stock exchanges. These are index-type ETF funds. As such, they try to generate returns equivalent to the indexes discussed below. This option does not consider investing in mutual bond funds.

OPTION 3

This is a bolder option. This strategy suggests investing all or a large portion of the savings that you have deposited in your pension fund (401k, IRA, ROTH, etc.) into a single indexed ETF fund that follows the SP500 index. There are several funds of this type, among which I can mention the following:

- SPDR SP500 ETF (SPY)

- IShares Core SP500 ETF (IVV)

- Vanguard SP500 ETF (VOO)

Investing in ETF SP500 is a proven investment strategy. Their average returns have been higher than that of mutual funds that are actively managed. Over the past 15 years, 92% of the active mutual funds have had lower returns than index funds that follow the SP500 index. According to Morningstar Inc. from 2007 to March 2017, investors transferred $1.1 trillion dollars from active mutual funds to indexed mutual funds.

Purchasing funds of SP500 ETF is also a strategy that allows you to benefit from all the advantages offered in general by mutual funds. This includes, as discussed above, diversification and distribution of risk, compounded accumulation of capital, tax deferred payments and in the case of ETF funds very low costs (0.05%) compared to ordinary mutual funds (1.5 to 2.3%) and the ability to buy and sell during the hours when the market is open (9:30 a.m. to 4 p.m.). This is compared to ordinary mutual funds which can be traded only at closing of the stock exchange normally at 4 pm. easter time.

Several reasons suggest this option:

Simplicity. In a single fund, an investor can buy, sell and control all his/her investments. This can easily be done from your computer. Once you enter your Schwab, Fidelity, Vanguard or any other financial institution account where you have your pension fund (401k, IRA, ROTH etc.), you can see the value of one SP500 mutual fund share in a window on your screen. From there you can move to a window to make a transaction (trade) and then you can choose if you want to buy or sell. You can do this at prices that the market has at that moment or you can set a limit to do a transaction. The screen will indicate the steps to follow until completing the transaction and printing the results.

Setting limits. When you set a "limit" to buy a share in the stock market what you are doing is giving an instruction about the maximum price that you are willing to buy. What happens is that when the price of the stock in the stock market goes down and reaches the limit, the system immediately proceeds to buy. If you want to sell, the instruction means the minimum price you are willing to sell. When the price of the stock rises and reaches the price limit, the system proceeds to sell at that price.

Saving growth. This system offers an excellent opportunity for *capital accumulation* by *long-term individual investors.* In a table above we showed an example of returns of six different savings and investment plans for a couple at 6% and 7% growth for 30 and 40 years.

The average return in the last 30 years of indexed ETF SP500 mutual funds has been 7% per annum, 2% corresponding to inflation and 5% to earnings. In that table a small percentage change in the rate of return produces a large difference in returns in the long term. Hence the importance of minimizing the costs charged to mutual funds.

Low costs. The costs charged by financial institutions in index funds have been falling in recent years due, in part, to the growing competition to attract the avalanche of retirees (called baby boomers), who need financial services to manage their retirement funds.

The annual management cost of an indexed fund can vary from 0.05% to 0.50% of the fund amount depending on the financial institution where you have your retirement fund. The total costs charged for the actively managed mutual funds fluctuate between 1.5% and 2.3%. This is a significant difference in cost and has a big impact on the total return of a fund.

This means that if an *ordinary or active mutual* fund declares an annual return of 9% you must discount the cost of administering it, which means you receive only 7% if the cost is 2%. So be alert when you receive written or spoken investment offers. In addition, for a 7% return if you subtract the inflation of 2% you have a real return of 5%. Now, if the fund is administered by a financial institution and not you directly, you must discount an additional 1%. This leaves you with a net return on your investment of 4%, 9% to 4% is a big difference. Be alert to these calculations.

In the case of *indexed funds*, at a 9% return you only must discount inflation (2%) and the management cost of the fund (0.05%). If it is administered by a financial institution one should discount an additional 1%, which leaves a total return for you of 4.95%. We already mentioned the significant impact that a small percentage change has on the long-term return of an investment. See tables above again.

Another advantage of this approach is that it is *easy to compare* these funds with other similar funds in relation to level of risk, return and price. This is because all the index funds based on the SP500 buy the same shares of the SP500 index. The slight variations between them are mostly due to the costs they charge for their administration.

Liquidity. The shares of these funds are easy to sell in the market and recover the money invested immediately. This is a very important factor.

Lower risk factor. The index funds based on the SP500 have great diversity in that they buy shares of the 500 largest corporations in the USA, which have the best administration and consistently the best profits and returns for investors. This diversity distributes the risk among all the qualified companies contained in the index. So, if some of them go down in price, others go up in price, which means that on average they compensate each other in fluctuations and generate in a positive relationship of growth of their values in the long term: between 7 and 9% historically.

There are several successful investors and finance specialists who recommend this type of investment, including John Bogle, founder of Vanguard Investments, who is considered the initiator of this type of investment. Another is Warren Buffet who has mentioned on several occasions that the best an individual private investor can do is to put his/her savings in an index fund for the long term.

SP500 corporations have been grouped into 11 sectors which represent almost all economic activity of the country, in different proportions according to the index definitions. These sectors are the following:

1. CONSUMER DISCRETIONAL (XLY)
2. CONSUMER STAPLES (XLP)
3. ENERGY (XLE)
4. FINANCIAL (XLF)
5. HEALTH CARE (XLV)
6. INDUSTRIAL (XLI)
7. MATERIALS (XLB)
8. REAL ESTATE (XLRE)
9. TECHNOLOGY (XLK)
10. UTILITIES (XLU)
11. TELECOMMUNICATION (XLC)

International diversity. An important factor to consider is that due to the size and nature of their activities, these corporations have extensive international activity (multinational) which means their profits, almost 40%, come from abroad.

Good capacity for recovery after a correction of the stock market. Historically, every year a correction or price decrease occurs in the stock market of about 10%. As discussed above, the recovery periods have been no longer than 3 months except when there are serious crises or a recession, such as the one of 2007-09. Once the levels prior to the correction have recovered, the shares have continued to rise. Larger corrections, such as the so-called "bear markets" where decreases in the stock market are 20% or more, have taken historically about five months to recover and then have risen to prior levels or beyond.

If the shares of these SP500 corporations fall in price on the stock market due to some economic crisis, it is likely that all other corporations on the national and international stock exchanges will be affected in one way or another. So, any place you have invested your savings will experience reduced value. In such a case, it seems preferable to be inside a SP500 indexed fund (be it a mutual fund or an ETF) that contains the best and largest corporations in the country and has a mayor political influence on the economy.

The important thing to consider when prices fall is that the Executives at the White House and Congress will be pressured by corporation managers and shareholders, especially those in the SP500, to adopt economic policies to reverse the situation as soon as possible. Politically, it is not possible to tolerate falling share prices for long because it affects all investors and has repercussions at national and international levels.

This is because the SP500 index is an important political indicator in addition to an economic indicator. The recovery of the stock market is of the highest interest for political leaders, especially when they consider their options in future elections. Employees (voters) now are shareholders through their pension funds such as 401k, IRA, ROTH and other similar systems and are constantly observing the behavior of the stock market because their financial future depends on it.

An example of election impact is what happened in the New York Stock Exchange (NYSE) when Mr. Trump was elected. Immediately, the NYSE had a notable rise in stock value and by the end of March 2017 had risen almost 19% from the day of the election. This extraordinary growth was due in large part to expectations of economic reforms promised during the presidential campaign. (Trump declared in 2019 that the stock exchange is a key indicator for his political future in 2020.)

TO REPEAT, the most important message to keep in mind for all portfolio options is that if the stock market falls, even 20% or more, do not sell the SP500 fund shares. Wait for the market to recover and reap the benefits of the market rise that will follow. Keep buying shares every month, in this case you will buy them at a lower price, which will greatly benefit your overall portfolio when the market recovers.

Finally, a further comment is worst making. We are living in a period of economic recovery with great uncertainty about the future. As of 2017 the new government offered a series of economic policy measures that helped the value of corporate shares rise based on expectations and promises of economic growth from these policies.

The most important thing is that whatever the new government policies are, you should not stop saving and investing in your pension and investment funds. If you invest monthly, you will be building an investment ladder that balances out the highs and lows of the market and generate historical nominal growth of around 7 to 9% per year. Try to do it automatically to avoid forgetfulness or negligence. Remember the opportunity cost of your income: what you stop spending on superfluous things or services you can invest in shares of your indexed fund.

Also consider other factors besides your investment portfolio. There may be needs of you and your spouse when you are close to retirement or once in retirement. For example, consider other investments you have: real estate (mainly your house, if it is paid or not), the amount that you and your spouse receive from Social Security, other types of pension or investments, an emergency account, your physical and health conditions, health insurance for long-term care, needing to help a family member economically, the lifestyle you want, the budget you will need during retirement.

ALTERNATIVE FUNDS

There are other funding strategies that could further simplify the investment decisions of an individual investor. In single funds, for example, you could have shares of U.S. corporations, international corporations, bonds and cash. The selection is made by the fund administration. Its annual costs are higher than that of ordinary indexed funds and ETFs. There are two types of funds that are worth mentioning: the so-called Balanced funds and the Target funds.

BALANCED FUNDS

One way to simplify your portfolio is to buy shares in a mutual fund that buys shares in corporations, bonds and money instruments. These funds are called balanced because they seek to maintain a diversification between stocks, bonds and cash according to a certain formula. The objective is to offer investors the diversification they need to minimize risk in a single fund. In this sense these funds are suitable for people who do not have the time, knowledge or inclination to make and monitor investments on their own.

The proportions vary between the different funds according to their objectives. Conservative funds have a proportion in shares of corporations that fluctuate between 30 and 50%. Normally these funds are attractive to people who are close to retirement and want less risk. Other funds have a more aggressive investment approach with up to 70 or 80% in shares, an approach attractive to investors who are beginning their working lives.

It is important to note that with balanced funds the decision to buy and sell financial instruments and determine the proportion between corporate stocks, bonds and money is the sole responsibility of the fund manager. You, as an investor, do not have the option to vary those ratios.

The return of balanced mutual funds has been lower than that of the indexed funds because their costs are higher, and the composition of their investments considers a higher proportion of bonds and cash, between 40% and 50%. Ten-year Treasury bond returns have fluctuated around 2%. The return of the cash instruments has been even lower, close to 0.13% (6 months), 0.25% (one year), 0.74% (5 years). For its part, the return of stock in indexed funds has been around 7 to 9%.

The annual cost of administering this type of balanced fund is higher than the cost of managing indexed funds. The former requires an administrative system, promotion, sale and monitoring and more elaborate information. Some costs are like those of active funds, despite close to 40% of their investments are in bonds, which usually have lower administration costs. The same applies regarding investments in money instruments such as certificate of deposits.

According to financial analysts the balanced funds with proportions of 60/40 have had historic returns of around 7.8% but have had costs of around 1.5% which makes the net return for the investor equivalent to 6.3%. (2% inflation and 3.3% return). Some of these funds are:

- Vanguard Balanced index (VBINX)
- Fidelity Balanced (FBALX)
- American Fund American Balance A (ABALX)
- Dodge / Cox Balanced (DODBX)

TARGET FUNDS

These funds are balanced, as explained above, but with an expiration date close to the year in which you wish to retire. These funds have begun to appear within 401k accounts opened by employers. The administrators of these accounts offer a variety of funds with various termination dates. Lately, employers have been automatically depositing contributions from employees (who have not chosen a type of investment) in a Target fund.

These funds are financially managed by professionals who determine the combination of stocks, bonds, cash or other forms of investment that the fund will include. A common way of doing this is by acquiring other mutual funds that meet the desired formula of investment for a given period of years.

The rationale for this special type of fund is that the employee transfers the investment decision to professionals because the employee considers that he/she does not have the knowledge, experience, inclination or ability to deal with risk. In addition, many employees believe that they do not have the discipline to make monthly contributions to their pension funds and prefer automatic deductions from their salary by the employer.

One of the advantages of these Target funds is that the managers change the investment formula as the years go by. For example, if you bought shares of a Target 2050 fund because you plan to retire in 2050, at the time of purchase the fund offers you a certain formula that in the first years is more aggressive or intensive in national and foreign corporate shares: 70% shares, 25% bonds and 5% cash with the promise of changing its composition to a more conservative or lower risk formula, 60/35/5, as you advance in years until you reach a low risk formula when you arrive to the retirement age, 30/65/5.

There are two types of Target funds: 1) those that end on the assigned date, which may be some years before retirement and 2) those that continue during the retirement period. The former type is more attractive to those who wish to liquidate their funds at that time and reinvest them in another form in accordance with their expectations, changing needs and opportunities. The latter type maintains or designs a more conservative formula that responds to the income needs of the person once in retirement.

The cost of these funds can be high, especially when they are made up of other funds. Not only are there costs of managing the Target fund (which can fluctuate around 1%) but also the costs of the mutual funds that have been included within the Target fund, which can be around .5% or more. A Target fund is mostly a fund of mutual funds. Some Target funds can be formed by more than 20 mutual funds and other investments.

Some Target funds are the following:

- Vanguard Target Retirement 2060 (VTTSX)

- Fidelity Freedom Target 2040 (FFFFX)

- Schwab Target 2040 (SWERX)

Finally, it is worth repeating that we are living through a period of economic recovery after the great recession of 2007-09. These are challenging years for the investor since there is uncertainty about the future when the economy has slow growth, around 2% per year. Even so, it has been possible to have rates of return close to 5% real returnin the US indexed funds.

RECOMMENDED READING

INTRODUCTION AND OVERVIEW

Vicki Robin and Joe Dominguez. Your Money or Your Life. Penguin Books. Revised edition 2008.

SOCIAL SECURITY AND MEDICARE

Publications from Social Security Administration and Medicare. 2018 and 2019

Davin Carroll. Social Security Basics. 9 Essentials that Everybody Should Know. Latest edition.

PENSION FUNDS

John C. Bogle. On Mutual Funds. New Perspectives for the Intelligent Investor. A dell Trade Paperback. Copyright 1994. Look for the latest edition.

Keith Dorney. Best Roth. A Beginner's Guide to Roth IRAs, Employer Roth Options, Conversions and Withdrawals. Keith Dorney Books. 2019.

Daniel R. Solin. The smarter 401(k) book you ever read: maximize your retirement saving. Penguin Group. 2018.

EMERGENCY FUNDS

Matt Nicholson. Building Your Emergency Funds. 2015.

DEBT MANAGEMENT

Richard Stanton. Debt Free. How to Get Out of Debt to Your Road Towards Financial Freedom. 2015.

Darren Hardy. The Compound Effect. Jump start your income, your life, your success. Da Capo Press. 2010.

James Clear. Atomic Habits. Penguin Random House. UK. 2018.

Jack Gray. Money Management. Discover how to get out of debt, create a budget, save money and make money while building real financial wealth. Great Reads Publishing. 2015.

HOUSE MORTGAGES

David Reed. Mortgage 101: quick answers to over 250 critical question about your home loan. 3rd Edition. American Management Association. 2018.

HEALTH CARE

Patrick Foley and Kristin Hillsley. Winning at Retirement. A guide to health, wealth, and purpose in the best years of your life. 2018.

EXTENDITURE STRATEGY

Emerys Westacott. The Wisdom of Frugality. Why less is more – more or less. Princeton University Press. 2016.

Chis Farrell. The New Frugality: how to consume less, save more and live better.

SAVING STRATEGY

Virginia B. Morris and Kenneth M. Morris. Guide to Saving for Retirement. Lightbulb Press. 2012.

Jane Dwinell. Freedom Through Frugality.

Ace McCloud. Saving Money. The top 100 best ways to save your money and spend your money wisely.

David Bach. The Automatic Millionaire. Broadway Books. 2014. Look for a later edition.

INVESTMENT STRATEGY

Virginia B. Morris and Kenneth M. Morris. Guide to Money and Investing. Lightbulb Press. 2012.

Gitman & Joehnk. Fundamentals of Investing. Addison Wesley. 2003. Look for a later edition

Burton G. Malkiel. A Random Walk Down Wall Street. W.W. Norton & Company. 2015. Look for the latest edition.

John C. Bogle. On Mutual Funds. New Perspectives for the Intelligent Investor. A dell Trade Paperback. 1994. Look for the latest edition.

OTHER RECOMMENDED READING

Benjamin Graham. The Intelligent Investor. HarperBusiness Book. Copyright 1973. Look for the later revised edition.

Charles R. Schwab. New Guide to Financial Independence. Practical solutions to busy people. Three Rives press. 2004.

Napoleon Hill. Think and Grow Rich. Fawcett Books. 1998. Look for the latest edition.

Grant Sabatier. Financial Freedom. A proven path to all the money you will ever need. Penguin Random House. 2019.

APPENDIX

STANDARD AND POOR BEGINNING OF THE YEAR MARKET CLOSING

SP 500 END OF THE YEAR CLOSING				SP 500 END OF THE YEAR CLOSING			
YEARS	CLOSING	YEARS	CLOSING	YEARS	CLOSING	YEARS	CLOSING
1-Jan-19		1-Jan-84	166.4	1-Jan-49	15.36	1-Jan-15	7.48
1-Jan-18	2,506.85	1-Jan-83	144.3	1-Jan-48	14.83	1-Jan-14	8.37
1-Jan-17	2,275.12	1-Jan-82	117.3	1-Jan-47	15.21	1-Jan-13	9.3
1-Jan-16	1,918.60	1-Jan-81	133	1-Jan-46	18.02	1-Jan-12	9.12
1-Jan-15	2,028.18	1-Jan-80	110.9	1-Jan-45	13.49	1-Jan-11	9.27
1-Jan-14	1,822.36	1-Jan-79	99.71	1-Jan-44	11.85	1-Jan-10	10.08
1-Jan-13	1,480.40	1-Jan-78	90.25	1-Jan-43	10.09	1-Jan-09	9.06
1-Jan-12	1,300.58	1-Jan-77	103.8	1-Jan-42	8.93	1-Jan-08	6.85
1-Jan-11	1,282.62	1-Jan-76	96.86	1-Jan-41	10.55	1-Jan-07	9.56
1-Jan-10	1,123.58	1-Jan-75	72.56	1-Jan-40	12.3	1-Jan-06	9.87
1-Jan-09	865.58	1-Jan-74	96.11	1-Jan-39	12.5	1-Jan-05	8.43
1-Jan-08	1,378.76	1-Jan-73	118.4	1-Jan-38	11.31	1-Jan-04	6.68
1-Jan-07	1,424.16	1-Jan-72	103.3	1-Jan-37	17.59	1-Jan-03	8.46
1-Jan-06	1,278.73	1-Jan-71	93.49	1-Jan-36	13.76	1-Jan-02	8.12
1-Jan-05	1,181.41	1-Jan-70	90.31	1-Jan-35	9.26	1-Jan-01	7.07
1-Jan-04	1,132.52	1-Jan-69	102	1-Jan-34	10.54	1-Jan-00	6.1
1-Jan-03	895.84	1-Jan-68	95.04	1-Jan-33	7.09	Jan 1, 1899	6.08
1-Jan-02	1,140.21	1-Jan-67	84.45	1-Jan-32	8.3	Jan 1, 1898	4.88
1-Jan-01	1,335.63	1-Jan-66	93.32	1-Jan-31	15.98	Jan 1, 1897	4.22
1-Jan-00	1,425.59	1-Jan-65	86.12	1-Jan-30	21.71	Jan 1, 1896	4.27
1-Jan-99	1,248.77	1-Jan-64	76.45	1-Jan-29	24.86	Jan 1, 1895	4.25
1-Jan-98	963.36	1-Jan-63	65.06	1-Jan-28	17.53	Jan 1, 1894	4.32
1-Jan-97	766.22	1-Jan-62	69.07	1-Jan-27	13.4	Jan 1, 1893	5.61
1-Jan-96	614.42	1-Jan-61	59.72	1-Jan-26	12.65	Jan 1, 1892	5.51
1-Jan-95	465.25	1-Jan-60	58.03	1-Jan-25	10.58	Jan 1, 1879	3.58
1-Jan-94	472.99	1-Jan-59	55.62	1-Jan-24	8.83	Jan 1, 1878	3.25
1-Jan-93	435.23	1-Jan-58	41.12	1-Jan-23	8.9	Jan 1, 1877	3.55
1-Jan-92	416.08	1-Jan-57	45.43	1-Jan-22	7.3	Jan 1, 1876	4.46
1-Jan-91	325.49	1-Jan-56	44.15	1-Jan-21	7.11	Jan 1, 1875	4.54
1-Jan-90	339.97	1-Jan-55	35.6	1-Jan-20	8.83	Jan 1, 1874	4.66
1-Jan-89	285.4	1-Jan-54	25.46	1-Jan-19	7.85	Jan 1, 1873	5.11
1-Jan-88	250.5	1-Jan-53	26.18	1-Jan-18	7.21	Jan 1, 1872	4.86
1-Jan-87	264.5	1-Jan-52	24.19	1-Jan-17	9.57	Jan 1, 1871	4.44
1-Jan-86	208.2	1-Jan-51	21.21	1-Jan-16	9.33		
1-Jan-85	171.6	1-Jan-50	16.88				

Made in United States
North Haven, CT
04 November 2026

21772015R00118